SHARLA FRITZ

Soul Spa

40 Days of Spiritual Renewal

CONCORDIA PUBLISHING HOUSE · SAINT LOUIS

To all the women who come to the Soul Spa
worn and tired, empty and hurting,
and to our precious Savior,
who promises to restore our souls with His grace.

Published 2015 by Concordia Publishing House
3558 S. Jefferson Avenue, St. Louis, MO 63118-3968
1-800-325-3040 · www.cph.org

Text © 2015 by Sharla Fritz

Unless otherwise indicated, Scripture quotations are from the ESV Bible® (The Holy Bible, English Standard Version®), copyright © 2001 by Crossway Bibles, a publishing ministry of Good News Publishers. Used by permission. All rights reserved.

Scripture quotations marked NASB taken from the New American Standard Bible®, Copyright © 1960, 1962, 1963, 1968, 1971, 1972, 1973, 1975, 1977, 1995 by The Lockman Foundation. Used by permission. (www.Lockman.org)

Scripture quotations marked KJV are from the King James or Authorized Version of the Bible.

Scripture quotations marked NIV are taken from the Holy Bible, New International Version®, NIV®. Copyright © 1973, 1978, 1984, 2011 by Biblica, Inc.™ Used by permission of Zondervan. All rights reserved worldwide. www.zondervan.com The "NIV" and "New International Version" are trademarks registered in the United States Patent and Trademark Office by Biblica, Inc.™

Manufactured in the United States of America

1   2   3   4   5   6   7   8   9   10   24   23   22   21   20   19   18   17   16   15

TABLE OF CONTENTS

INTRODUCTION

Imagine opening your mailbox and discovering a lovely red envelope inside addressed to you. You rip it open and find an invitation to a health spa not far from your home. The invitation informs you that someone has anonymously purchased an all-inclusive two-night stay for you. "Come," the letter says. "Enjoy our delicious and healthful food, experience a relaxing massage, refresh your skin with a luxurious facial, try the myriad of fitness classes we offer, and spend some time soaking in the pool or hot tub. Everything is provided for you. All you need to do is book your stay."

Sounds good, right? With our crazy busy lives, a weekend to relax sounds heavenly. As women, we often spend more time taking care of others than ourselves. A little pampering would be nice. Household chores, yard work, and lifting little ones all take a toll on our bodies. A stay at a spa would refresh our aching muscles.

To prepare for the writing of this book, I spent a couple of days at a health spa. I know. Tough work, but somebody had to do it. At the spa, I ate Southwest-style wrap sandwiches, spinach quiche, and chocolate soufflé. An expert massage therapist rubbed the tension out of my muscles. I took a water aerobics class and tried a few Pilates exercises. I had a manicure while looking out the window at a peaceful pond. When I left the spa, my body felt refreshed.

I would have liked to send each of you an invitation to join me at the spa. What a blast that would have been! Unfortunately, that isn't in my budget. But I would like to invite you to a different kind of spa—a Soul Spa. Instead of traveling to a posh hotel or country resort, you will stay right where you are. Instead of massages and facials designed to restore your body, you will engage in experiences that renew your soul.

At this spa, you will learn to take care of the most important part of you. We don't always think about soul upkeep. After all, we feel the aches in our muscles. Touching our dry skin reveals its need for cleansing and moisturizing. Our stomach growls when it's empty. But we can't see our soul. We don't hear its cries of hunger. We may sense something is wrong, but we rarely slow down long enough to assess the pain of an aching heart.

So, come to the Soul Spa. Learn how to care for your soul through renewing habits and practices. Perhaps you already participate in some of these practices, such as Bible study, prayer, worship, Christian service, and the Lord's Supper. But maybe you don't consider them to be soul maintenance. You enjoy them, they are part of your life, but they do not always refresh your soul.

Other holy habits we will consider may be new to you. Scripture meditation, SACRED reading, examen, solitude, secrecy, and fasting are also means of soul renewal. Think of each of these practices as a room in the Soul Spa where God is waiting for you, eager to meet with you and care for your spirit. He will soothe your hurts and inspire you with hope. He will rub out the effects of constricting sins and free your heart with love. He will meet you in His Word and fill your spirit with joy.

At the Soul Spa, you will find a variety of practices for the health of your spirit. Week One will introduce the topic of soul care. Each of the following weeks will explore a category of spiritual habits outlined by the words *Soul Spa*.

Study: Practices that get us into God's Word

Open: Practices that unlock the heart to God's leading

Uplift: Practices that connect us with God in worship

Loosen: Practices that allow us to approach God without pretense

Share: Practices that involve the Body of Christ

Pray: Practices that enable us to call out to God

Attune: Practices that help us arrange our lives to meet God

The readings begin with an exploration of how Jesus used these practices while He was here on earth. He modeled how to live in this hectic, messy, and complicated world with grace. He continually kept in contact with the Father even as He touched the lives of needy human beings.

Other readings examine various soul habits. You will get a small taste of twenty-eight different experiences. At first, this may seem overwhelming. Just as a health spa menu offers a myriad of massage and exercise options, the Soul Spa introduces many ways to take care of your soul, but don't be alarmed. You aren't expected to engage in all of them at the same time.

At a health resort, you might try every option available but discover a Swedish massage and a chamomile facial are exactly what your body craves right now. Here at the Soul Spa, you will probably find that certain practices meet your soul's genuine needs better than others. At the end of our spa experience, you will learn how to create your own soul care plan, picking and choosing from the Soul Spa "menu."

Each day includes a reading, questions to ponder, and an investigation into God's Word. Dig deep into Scripture. Memorize the week's theme verse and allow God's Word to transform your mind.

Check out the Spa Session activities each week. These activities help you to go deeper into the Soul Spa experience. I encourage you to circle the ones that most appeal to you and make time in your schedule to sample at least one of these methods of soul care.

I've also included suggestions for "visiting" the Soul Spa with a group. Have fun creating a bit of a spa atmosphere wherever you are meeting. Discuss the weekly readings and Soul Study questions. Allow each woman to choose one question that speaks to her heart. After she gives her answer, open up that question to the other members of the group. The leader may also want to highlight important questions or comments not brought up by the group. After discussing the week's readings and Bible studies, you will have the opportunity to try one of the week's practices together.

As I write this, I am praying for each of you. Praying this study will lead you to a greater intimacy with your Lord and Savior. Hoping you will discover ways to become more aware of God's nearness to you in the middle of your hectic life. Praying you will hear the Father's whispers of love to you during ordinary days.

Let's open the door of the spa together.

WELCOME TO THE SOUL SPA

Have you ever longed to go to a place where you could forget about your day-to-day problems for a while? Where you would be pampered with facials and manicures? Where expert chefs would prepare special-order orange-glazed salmon and chocolate soufflés for you? Where therapists would massage the stress out of your knotted muscles?

Then a visit to a luxury spa might be just what you are looking for. There you could relax by the pool or get a massage. You could visit the sauna or the gym. You could sleep in or take an early morning walk. At the spa, you can do whatever you need to do to restore a weary body.

During the next eight weeks, we will be visiting a different kind of spa—a Soul Spa. Because even though taking care of our bodies is important, caring for our souls is even more crucial. In these pages, you will discover a center for your spirit. As you encounter the God of restoration in the rooms of this spa, He will touch your heart. This week, I will introduce you to the topic of soul care and the practices that can revitalize your spirit. You will discover meaningful ways to connect with God and focus on His constant and merciful presence in your life. In the Soul Spa, God will meet you, take your weary soul, and give it new life.

Are you ready? Step through the spa doors.

I pray the Lord my soul to keep.

From a child's prayer

MEMORY VERSE

*He restores my soul. He leads me in paths
of righteousness for His name's sake.*
Psalm 23:3

SOUL TIRED

Discipline yourself for the purpose of godliness.
1 Timothy 4:7b NASB

I came to the spa totally spent.

I needed to recharge after a whirlwind summer. During that short season, I taught weekly piano lessons, started a new book, and scheduled new speaking engagements. My son got married to a wonderful young woman, and my daughter and her family traveled from China to attend the wedding and to visit us for two months.

These were all wonderful things, but now I was tired. And not the kind of tired one good night's sleep would cure. I was deeply tired. So I checked myself into a spa for some extended relaxation. I hoped a little pampering would rejuvenate my weary body and mind.

By this point in my life, I know myself pretty well. I know that when I'm so tired my bones ache, I need to crawl under the covers earlier than usual. When I get that annoying crick in my neck, I crave my husband's expert neck rubs. When my hip starts to go out on me, I need to do a crazy-looking, but effective exercise that gets it back into the right position.

I am also able to diagnose a few emotional ills as well. When I'm starting to sound like Eeyore with a pity-poor-me attitude, I realize I've been too isolated. Lunch with a friend is a necessity. When I seem to snap at everything my husband says, I prescribe myself time alone with a good book. When my heart feels desiccated and squeezed dry, I know I need a walk in the woods.

But sometimes I try all of my usual remedies and still feel empty. I sample a recommended dose of each treatment and still experience a cavernous vacuum inside. It's then I realize that I'm soul tired.

But where do we go when our spirit is weary? What do we do when our soul aches?

We can't take our spirits out of our bodies and send them to a massage therapist. We can't direct our souls to a good Pilates instructor who is able to rejuvenate them.

However, we can bring our exhausted, fatigued, and shattered souls to the Father who promises to restore them. The God of the universe alone is able to renew or revitalize our spirits. So we come to Him.

One method to approach the God of renovation is through a series of exercises that open our hearts to Him. The apostle Paul talks about these practices in 1 Timothy 4:7:

> But have nothing to do with worldly fables fit only for old women. On the other hand, discipline yourself for the purpose of godliness. (NASB)

The Greek word for discipline in this passage is *gymnazo*, which means "to exercise vigorously, in any way, either the body or the mind."[1] In the New Testament, *gymnazo* is translated as "exercise," "train," or "discipline." In 1 Timothy 4:7, Paul is encouraging us to engage in spiritual practices that develop our relationship with God in the same way that physical training strengthens our muscles.

For centuries, devout Christians yearning for a deeper relationship with God have used exercises called Spiritual disciplines. These Spiritual disciplines are not discipline in the sense of punishment. They are not disciplines in the sense of tedious, repetitive calisthenics. They are disciplines in the way of training our souls to see God more clearly.

These practices are not magic formulas that instantly make us super-Christians. They don't work automatically. They do require faith. But these faith practices become habits that help us see God more clearly and respond to His love. Scripture meditation and Bible study are how I hear God's voice. Solitude and silence enable me to shut out all the other distracting voices.

When I went to the spa, I relaxed, read a book, had a massage, exercised, and slept. I could have done all of those things at home (enlisting my husband for a back rub), but most likely I wouldn't have. Instead my type-A personality would have heard the grimy shower walls pleading to be scrubbed, the overflowing in-box screaming to be organized, and the clothes in the stuffed-to-the-max hamper begging to be washed. Intentionally going to the spa helped me ignore those other necessary jobs for a time so I could concentrate on what my body needed.

In the same way, purposely practicing the Spiritual disciplines enables us to care for our souls and spirits. They open us to God's working in our lives, giving Him the time and space to tend to our hearts. They provide a framework for our faith to receive God's grace.

Gymnazo literally means to exercise naked and was only used to describe the professional combat sports like boxing and wrestling. Athletes participated in these sports without clothing for greater freedom of movement and to prevent any advantage an opponent might obtain in grabbing their clothes.[2] Listen ladies, I'm glad to wear my yoga pants! But we may need to strip off wrong attitudes or superfluous activities that grasp a hold on our lives in order to achieve the goal of godliness.

Part of the beauty of going to a spa is that everything is done for you. Expert chefs cook your meals. Massage therapists work out your kinks. Aestheticians clarify your skin.

That same beauty exists in the Spiritual disciplines. Think of them as the spa you attend to experience God's transformational touch. Through the Confession and Absolution, He clarifies your spirit. Through Bible study and the Lord's Supper, He feeds your soul with heavenly food.

Is your soul tired? Does your spirit ache for more? Use the Spiritual disciplines to open uninterrupted time and quiet space to receive God's gifts as He speaks to you through His Word. He will transform your weary heart. As you meet God in the various rooms of this spa, He will miraculously touch your heart and heal your soul. You will discover your truest desires and deepest longings and find Him to be the satisfaction of them all.

Heavenly Father, my soul is weary. I need Your touch. Show me how to pay attention to the condition of my spirit and to turn to You for healing. Teach me about new habits and disciplines that will open me to Your presence in my life. Transform me. In Jesus' name. Amen.

Day One

Soul Study

1. Have you ever been to a spa? What did the experience do for your body and mind?

2. When you are physically tired, what do you do to take care of your body?

3. What do you do for yourself when you feel emotionally drained?

4. Today we learned about the Greek word *gymnazo*. Look up these other verses that use this word. Read the whole passage, and then concentrate on the sentence printed below that contains the word translated from *gymnazo* in bold print. What do you discover about the meaning of *gymnazo* from these verses?

    a. Hebrews 5:11–14 (Instruction for spiritual maturity)

> "But solid food is for the mature, for those who have their powers of discernment **trained** by constant practice to distinguish good from evil" (v. 14).

b. Hebrews 12:7–11 (Most of the words translated as "discipline" in this passage are from the Greek word *paideia*, which means "chastisement or instruction.")

> "For the moment all discipline seems painful rather than pleasant, but later it yields the peaceful fruit of righteousness to those who have been **trained** by it" (v. 11).

c. 2 Peter 2:12–14 (This passage is describing false teachers.)

> "They have eyes full of adultery, insatiable for sin. They entice unsteady souls. They have hearts **trained** in greed" (v. 14).

d. In light of these passages and the way they use the word *gymnazo*, write "Discipline yourself for the purpose of godliness" in your own words.

5. Write out this week's memory verse.

Spa Session

The goal of a visit to the Soul Spa is to become more aware of God's constant loving presence in our lives. Sometime this week, carve out space in your schedule to try one of these activities to draw you into the presence of the Lord.

☼ Look up the following verses about God's abiding presence: Exodus 33:14; Deuteronomy 31:8; Psalm 73:23; Isaiah 41:10; Matthew 28:20; and Hebrews 13:5b. Choose two or three that are especially meaningful to you. Write these verses on cards to carry with you through the day. Read them in small moments of the day to help you remember God is with you now. At the end of the week, write about the effect of this exercise on your life.

☼ Consider the omnipresence of the Almighty. Look at some amazing photographs of space from the Hubble telescope (http://hubblesite. org/gallery/album). Consider the words of Psalm 147:2–4, and praise the God who knows each star by name but still cares about your broken heart.

☼ Music is a powerful way to enter the presence of God. Listen to a contemporary song like "So Come" by Israel & New Breed or "Here" by Kari Jobe. Or sing a hymn like "Abide with Me," "God Himself Is Present," or "Abide, O Dearest Jesus." Thank God that He is always with you.

☼ Psalm 95:2 says, "Let us come into His presence with thanksgiving; let us make a joyful noise to Him with songs of praise!" An attitude of thanksgiving ushers into an awareness of God's nearness. Make a thank-You card for God. It could be simple or artistic, full of poetic words, or an unadorned list of blessings. As you create the card, be aware God is right there with you. Offer your words of praise and thanksgiving to the Lord who is near.

Write about your experience here or in a journal.

INTIMACY WITH GOD

*Bodily discipline is only of little profit, but godliness
is profitable for all things, since it holds promise
for the present life and also for the life to come.*
1 Timothy 4:8 NASB

Imagine this fictional advertisement:

> Come to the Soul Spa to deepen your relationship with God.
> In each room of the spa, your Savior will accept you with open
> arms and lavish you with love. Christ will take your weary
> and tired soul and, in His presence, give it new life.

I don't know about you, but if there were a resort like that anywhere on earth, I would want to book a yearlong stay as soon as possible. My exhausted soul could use some renewal. My spirit longs to meet my Messiah.

Unfortunately, there is no tangible vacation spot for our souls. I can't send my spirit for a week at "Sandals for Souls." I can't book a cruise for my soul on Royal Caribbean. And even if I could, after one week, my soul would once again be stuck in a routine that sprints through life, rarely stopping to take a breath.

That's why we must take time out of our frenzied, chaotic lives to care for our souls. That's the reason it's essential to establish small habits that enable us to meet with the Soul Healer.

I didn't always view practices like Bible study and prayer as soul care. At times in my life, I viewed them as duties. Or requirements. Or even as a way to be a super-Christian. Read a few chapters of Romans and spend some time in intercession for the world and get a few gold stars on your spiritual report card. Try a little harder with fasting or Scripture meditation and maybe get a heavenly A+.

Of course, this is a ridiculous notion. Yet Satan, as well as our own sinful human nature, continues to subtly push lies like this: The more you do for God, the more acceptable He will find you.

A visit to the Soul Spa will not give you a higher religious rank or cushier corner office up in heaven. The reason we pursue Bible study and prayer, Scripture memorization and solitude is to draw closer to God. When Paul was writing to his protégé, Timothy, he outlined the purpose of a life of Spiritual discipline:

> Discipline yourself for the purpose of godliness; for bodily discipline is only of little profit, but godliness is profitable for all things, since it holds promise for the present life and *also* for the *life* to come. 1 Timothy 4:7b–8 NASB

We discipline ourselves for the purpose of godliness. The word *godliness* comes from the Greek word *eusebia*, which means "directed reverence and external piety."[3] It denotes reverence and respect. Spiritual disciplines lead us to a deeper reverence for God. They give us an eternal perspective.

The apostle Peter used the word *eusebia* in his second letter:

> His divine power has granted to us all things that pertain to life and godliness, through the knowledge of Him who called us to His own glory and excellence. 2 Peter 1:3

Godliness is a gift. We cannot even worship or be reverent in our own power. But it is also something we strive toward. Peter continues:

> For this very reason, make every effort to supplement your faith with virtue, and virtue with knowledge, and knowledge with self-control, and self-control with steadfastness, and steadfastness with godliness, and godliness with brotherly affection, and brotherly affection with love. 2 Peter 1:5–7

Because this world will continually attempt to crowd out God, we must make an effort in our life of faith. It is necessary to train ourselves for the purpose of godliness. As we intentionally make space and time in our lives to meet with God, He leads us to a deeper appreciation of His boundless power, grace, and love. He cares for our weary souls, pulling them closer to His heart.

Training ourselves involves our bodies. We are not entirely spiritual beings. In the Book of Romans, the apostle Paul tells us, "Present your bodies as a living sacrifice, holy and acceptable to God, which is your spiritual worship" (Romans 12:1). These disciplines of the Spirit are ways to offer our bodies as living sacrifices. Fasting, Holy Communion, and service involve our physical selves. Using our minds to memorize Scripture and intentionally placing ourselves in solitude are ways we can surrender bodily.

We don't do these things as punishment or in an effort to make us more acceptable to God. Faith in Christ's sacrifice on the cross is the only way to be acceptable in God's sight. Instead, presenting our bodies as living sacrifices through Spiritual disciplines is an act of worship. These practices are conduits for gracious transformation. Through them, we put ourselves in a place where God can rub out the effects of living in this world and renew our minds.

So why read the Bible or spend time in prayer? Why practice confession or solitude or hospitality? Not to get an A on your spiritual report card. Not to impress the church crowd. Not to be more ordered and systematic in your devotional life. Practice Spiritual disciplines to experience a deeper reverence of God and to be transformed in His presence.

Come to the Soul Spa to meet with your Savior. Carve out some time in your calendar for soul upkeep. Let Christ renew your weary spirit.

Heavenly Father, I confess sometimes I read my Bible, pray, and worship out of duty. Sometimes, I do it because I want people to think I am spiritual. But, Lord, I want to learn a new way of doing things. I want to offer my body as a living sacrifice so You can transform me. Lead me to a new level of reverence for Your work in my life. Amen.

Day Two

Soul Study

1. The apostle Paul wrote, "Discipline yourself for the purpose of godliness; for bodily discipline is only of little profit, but godliness is profitable for all things" (1 Timothy 4:7b–8 NASB). Think about bodily discipline. If you are able, engage in a few physical exercises: do some abdominal crunches, pump a few push-ups, or run in place. How did the exercise affect your body? What do you gain from a long-term physical training program?

2. Now think about exercises we do for our spirits. Look at the list below and circle the ones that you already engage in.

Bible reading	Confession	Scripture memorization	Meditation
Service	Simplicity	Hospitality	Solitude
Prayer	Examen	Worship	Fasting

Choose one that you circled. Write about how engaging in that activity affects your life.

Choose one that you didn't circle. What would your life look like if you made more time for that practice?

3. Read Romans 12:1–2.
   a. Paul instructs us to *present* our bodies as living sacrifices. The Greek word is *paristēmi*, which means "to place or set before someone." Other versions translate it as "offer," "give," or "dedicate." Think of some ways you can *paristēmi* your body to God.

b. In the Old Testament, believers were to sacrifice animals to atone for sins. The animals were killed on the altar. Paul asks us to offer our bodies as *living* sacrifices. Which sacrificial system, in your opinion, is more difficult—the Old Testament way or the New Testament way? Why?

c. Paul urges us not to be conformed to the pattern of the world. What tactics does the world use to conform you to its pattern (example: television commercials)? Place an asterisk next to the tactics you most struggle against.

d. Instead of conforming to the world, we are to be transformed. The whole purpose of the Spiritual disciplines is to allow God the time and space to transform us. Next to each of the world's tactics in Question 3c, write down the Spiritual discipline (from Question 2) you think would be the most effective in fighting against it.

4. Write out this week's memory verse.

Day Three

RECEIVING

We have fixed our hope on the living God, who
is the Savior of all men, especially of believers.
1 Timothy 4:10 NASB

Candles flickered in the dim light. Pleasant yet exotic scents wafted through the air. Soft music filled the room.

I entered the space wearing . . . a fluffy white bathrobe.

I was about to experience my first massage by a real massage therapist. The luxury spa was part of the posh hotel where I and a group of women were attending a retreat. I was the speaker that weekend, and the organizers of the event had graciously given me a gift certificate for the spa's services.

So I decided to enjoy a real massage. Having the tension in my neck and shoulders unraveled sounded heavenly. All I had to do was lie down on the massage table, listen to the calming music, and relax. The massage therapist took care of the rest. I couldn't help her do her job by jumping up and saying, "Let me take care of that kink!" A massage was not something I could do for myself. It was a gift I needed to receive.

In the same way, our spirituality is not something we can do for ourselves. It is a gift of God that we receive. John Kleinig writes in his book *Grace Upon Grace*, "Our whole life as the children of God is a life of reception."[4] We want to take the credit for our spiritual growth. There is a temptation to think that a certain repetition of prayers or a definite number of days spent fasting will make us stronger Christians. After all, twelve reps of bicep curls a day make for more powerful arms.

But the Spiritual habits we will be exploring are much more like going to a spa than going to a gym. We read the Bible, meditate, and pray to put ourselves in a position to receive what God offers us by His grace.

Let's look a little further at our focus passage in 1 Timothy 4:

> Discipline yourself for the purpose of godliness; for bodily
> discipline is only of little profit, but godliness is profitable
> for all things, since it holds promise for the present life and
> *also* for the *life* to come. It is a trustworthy statement deserving
> full acceptance. For it is for this we labor and strive, because
> we have fixed our hope on the living God, who is the Savior
> of all men, especially of believers (vv. 7–10 NASB).

Paul encourages us to put ourselves into a training regimen, but on our own we cannot make ourselves godly. It is only because "we have fixed our hope on the living God" that we can expect to be transformed. The word *hope* in Greek is *elpezo*, which means "to wait for salvation with joy and full confidence."[5] I love that! I can come to the spiritual spa fully expecting God to meet me there. He will cleanse my heart and lovingly work out the kinks in my soul.

In his letter to the Colossians, Paul wrote,

> Therefore, as you received Christ Jesus the Lord, so walk in Him,
> rooted and built up in Him and established in the faith, just as
> you were taught, abounding in thanksgiving. Colossians 2:6–7

There is nothing we can do to save ourselves. The Holy Spirit even gives us the faith to receive Jesus as our Savior and Lord. In the same way, we cannot make ourselves grow in faith, we can only receive heart change as a gift from God. Kleinig puts it this way:

> Our spirituality does not come from having spiritual powers
> or from our spiritual self-development but depends on our faith
> in Him. Because we are joined to Christ we continually receive
> our life from Him.[6]

Just as the massage at the luxury spa was a gift from the retreat organizers and the massage therapist, our spirituality—our life in Christ—is a gift from God.

However, we can't ignore the gift. When the retreat organizers gave me the valuable gift certificate to the spa, I could have thrown it away. I could have told myself I didn't need any of the spa's services. If I had shunned even the effort it took to walk to the spa, I would not have received the massage.

We can't make ourselves more godly or more spiritual, but when I ignore my Father's invitation to a deeper relationship with Him, my spirit suffers. When I tell myself I don't need God in my everyday life, my soul withers. When I don't make the effort to meet with my Savior, my heart weakens. However, when I do cooperate with the Holy Spirit—my Spiritual Director—He works in my heart to lead me to a deeper relationship with God.

Of course, it is not Spiritual disciplines themselves that transform us. In our modern fast-paced world, people are seeking spirituality in solitude and silence. They are trying to discover meaning in this materialistic age through simplicity and service. Journaling and meditation have become avenues for self-discovery. But without the work of the Holy Spirit, they are only lifeless self-improvement projects that ultimately reveal only our human shortcomings, hopeless efforts, and fleeting existence.

Christian spirituality is an ordinary life of faith where we receive the extraordinary. Practicing Spiritual disciplines doesn't take us away from our everyday existence; it helps us to see God's holy presence in our commonplace events.

We receive God's love in our ordinary moments and say thank You.

Holy Spirit, thank You for the gift of faith You have so graciously given me. Forgive me when I ignore Your calls to a deeper life or when I mistakenly think I can manage on my own. Open my heart to see You working in my life. Thank You that I can come to You fully expecting Your bountiful gifts of grace and love. In Jesus' name. Amen.

Day Three

Soul Study

1. Which of these scenarios most describes your spiritual life?

    a. Jumping off the massage table to try to do it myself

    b. Ignoring the spa gift certificate and not showing up for its services

    c. Telling myself I don't need any of the spa's services

    d. Informing the spa director he's doing it all wrong and insisting on my way

    e. Making the effort to go to the spa and receive what I need

2. What is your reaction to the statement "Our whole life as the children of God is a life of reception"?

3. It is only because "we have fixed our hope on the living God" (1 Timothy 4:10 NASB) that we can expect to be transformed. The word *hope* in Greek is *elpezo*, which means "to wait for salvation with joy and full confidence."

    a. In a few sentences, describe a child who is waiting for his or her parent with full confidence.

    b. Now describe a child who is waiting for his or her parent, but without confidence the parent will show up.

    c. Which child are you?

    d. At times, we all act like the child without confidence. Look up the following verses and describe why we can fix our hope on the living God. Circle the one that most inspires your hope in God today. Write it on a card to carry with you or post in a prominent place.
    Deuteronomy 31:6
    Psalm 136:1
    Psalm 23:1

4. Write out this week's memory verse.

YEARNING TO KNOW HIM BETTER

In speech, conduct, love, faith and purity,
show yourself an example of those who believe.
1 Timothy 4:12 NASB

When I first discovered the Spiritual disciplines, I thought I had stumbled upon a new practice. Sure, Bible study and prayer had been part of my life since I was young. I knew people who fasted. I worshiped in church on Sundays. But I had never heard of the practice called examen (I thought someone just didn't know how to spell). I had totally lost the art of Sabbath. And I had never thought of service and hospitality as ways to mature in faith.

But as I studied the Spiritual disciplines, I learned that they had been around for centuries. In fact, these outward expressions of maturing faith have existed for millennia. Many of the disciplines are derived from Jesus' life on earth as a faithful Son. He demonstrated the need for solitude by often retreating to lonely places to spend time with His Father. Before He began His earthly ministry, He fasted for forty days and nights, demonstrating His readiness to begin His earthly ministry. On the night before His crucifixion, He stooped down to wash the disciples' dusty feet, modeling service to others.

People of the Early Church also used these disciplines. Acts 2:42 tells us that the believers "devoted themselves to the apostles' teaching and the fellowship, to the breaking of bread and the prayers." They engaged in the disciplines of study and prayer. The breaking of bread could refer to Holy Communion or the practice of hospitality. The early believers observed fixed hours of prayer (Acts 3:1). Service was regarded as a spiritual ministry (Acts 6). Fasting was one of their spiritual habits (Acts 14:23).

The *Didache* is an early Christian text that described the way of life and the way of death. The way of life is to love God and love your neighbor as yourself. This book instructed believers in the disciplines of fasting, prayer, stewardship, and the Lord's Supper.

In the third and fourth centuries, there was a movement of Christian hermits and monks who retreated into the deserts of Egypt in order to grow closer to God. These Desert Fathers, as they are called, longed to be conformed to the image of Christ and so regularly practiced the disciplines of silence, solitude, contemplation, and detachment. They began to form monastic communities that ordered their lives with the disciplines of fixed-hour prayer, memorization, service, simplicity, and meditation.[7]

In the sixteenth century, the Reformation brought about spiritual change. Bible study and intercessory prayer were encouraged for all people, not just for the religious elite.[8] Luther made a point of making spirituality accessible to everyone. He wrote an enlightening booklet on prayer that was addressed not to monks in the abbey, but to his barber.[9] He set the words of his hymns to current popular tunes.

Luther practiced a form of the Spiritual discipline known as *Lectio Divina* or Divine Reading. In this ancient way of meditating on Scripture, Luther taught three rules for studying the theology of a passage. The first step was *Oratio*—praying for humility and openness to the Holy Spirit's teaching. *Meditatio* came next—reading and meditating on God's Word. Third, there was *Tentatio*, or temptation—seeing how the wisdom of Scripture addressed the temptations of life.[10] This method enabled the spiritual pilgrim to read and apply God's Word to his or her personal struggles.

Through the years, the disciplines of prayer, worship, confession, service, study of the Word, and participation in the Lord's Supper have been conduits of God's love. Throughout the ages, they have been a way to spend time with Jesus. In Christ's presence, we are able to confront our hidden fears, uncover our deepest desires, and face our greatest temptations.

We don't need to hole ourselves up in a monastery to practice these Spiritual disciplines. These habits are not only for those who retreat to a desert to focus on God. In Jesus' time, a rabbi was very selective about whom he chose as his pupils. A great teacher chose only those students who showed sufficient promise as students. Yet Jesus didn't choose men who had already dedicated their lives to religion. He didn't select followers with great education or reputation. Instead, He taught Scripture interpretation to simple fishermen. He trained shunned tax collectors how to pray. Habits designed to deepen our relationship to God are for everyone.

Just as other rabbis probably questioned Jesus' choice in disciples, perhaps Paul's colleagues voiced reservations when the apostle chose young Timothy as a protégé. He wrote to Timothy:

> Prescribe and teach these things. Let no one look down on your youthfulness, but *rather* in speech, conduct, love, faith *and* purity, show yourself an example of those who believe. Until I come, give attention to the *public* reading of *Scripture,* to exhortation and teaching. 1 Timothy 4:11–13 NASB

Although Timothy was young, Paul asked him to discipline himself for the purpose of godliness. Timothy was to set an example for all believers. His speech and conduct, his love and faith were to model Christ. Through the reading of Scripture, he was to encourage and teach. Spiritual practices are for the young and old.

A deep relationship with God is not only for spiritual elitists. It is not just for those who make their living writing sermons and teaching Bible studies. It's for those of us who deal with cranky customers and obstinate kids. It's for those who work with ringing telephones and recalcitrant computers. Spiritual practices performed in the middle of our mundane days bring us into the presence of an astonishing God. Simple sacred habits can transform chaotic homes into sanctuaries of peace.

The only prerequisites to a deeper life with Christ are the yearning to know Him better and the willingness to open yourself to the Spirit's work in your life. Our Savior is waiting for us with open arms, ready to draw us closer to Him. The Spiritual disciplines by themselves are not a magic formula for a holy, pious life, but they can be a way to open ourselves to God's invitation to a profound, hidden, multifaceted connection to Him.

Father in heaven, thank You for the examples of saints through the ages who have led others to a deeper walk with You. Help me in my journey with You. Grant Your Holy Spirit to lead me to follow You without reservation. In Jesus' name. Amen.

Soul Study

1. The Spiritual disciplines have been used through the centuries to connect in a deeper way with God. Close your eyes for a minute and think about these questions: What do you want your relationship with God to look like? What is missing in your spiritual life? What do you hope to gain through these forty days of spiritual renewal? Journal your answer here:

2. Psalm 84 is the deeply felt song of a person yearning for God. Read the psalm and consider these questions.

   a. How can you tell the psalmist is yearning for God (vv. 1–3)?

   b. What word pictures does he use to express this longing?

   c. According to the psalm, who is blessed (vv. 4–7)?

d. Verse 5 talks about those "whose hearts are set on pilgrimage" (NIV) or those "whose heart are the highways to Zion" (ESV). The Israelites took regular pilgrimages to Jerusalem (Zion) to meet with God. Examine your heart right now. Do the well-traveled roads lead to God or something else?

e. How do the words of verses 10–12 inspire a desire for a closer walk with Christ?

3. Write out this week's memory verse.

Day Five

INSIDE AND OUT

Pay close attention to yourself and to your teaching;
persevere in these things. 1 Timothy 4:16 NASB

A smiling senior citizen opened the door and let us in. His cropped white hair was a stark contrast against his chocolate-brown skin. He shuffled into his dining room and motioned my husband and me to follow.

"There it is," he announced, pointing to a twenty-year-old Wurlitzer. "It was my wife's piano, but she's been gone these ten years and no one plays it anymore. It's time it goes to a new home."

I ran my hand over the beautiful mahogany finish and pictured his wife carefully polishing the piano every week. *Surely, this piano was loved.*

But when I sat down on the bench and tentatively played a few scales, I cringed. *Ouch. Every note was out of tune.*

"When was the piano last tuned?" I asked. *I think I already know the answer.*

"Oh, I don't know," he said. "It's been awhile. But this here piano is just like new. Not a 150 songs been played on it."

Cute—thinking songs on a piano are like miles on a car.

Although the price was right and I desperately needed a piano to practice on, my husband and I weren't sure we should buy it. After all, the outside of the instrument had been cared for, but the inside—the part that mattered—had not. Could the piano be brought back to playing condition? Could a little care renovate it to function for its original purpose?

Many of us are like that twenty-year-old Wurlitzer. We spend time taking care of the outside. We go to the hair salon for a cut and color. We sign up for fitness classes. We shop for fashionable clothes.

But we often neglect the important part—the inside.

Paul instructed his protégé, Timothy, "Pay close attention to yourself." Was Paul instructing Timothy to pay attention to the way he looked or to his physical abilities? From the passages we have already looked at, we can see that is not the case. Earlier in the chapter, Paul tells the young pastor "bodily discipline is only of little profit, but godliness is profitable for all things" (1 Timothy 4:8 NASB). Although taking care of our bodies is important, Paul was encouraging Timothy to pay attention to his spiritual part—the part that would live on eternally.

Jesus also talked about paying attention to the soul:

> For what will it profit a man if he gains the whole world and forfeits his soul? Or what shall a man give in return for his soul?
> Matthew 16:26

What is the soul, anyway? The Greek word used for "soul" in Matthew 16 is *psyche*, which means "the vital force which animates the body" and "the seat of feelings, desires, affections."[11] The soul is the part of us that is eternal. It is that element of ourselves that yearns, loves, and makes decisions. John Ortberg, author of the book *Soul Keeping*, writes:

> The soul is the coolest, eeriest, most mysterious, evocative, sacred, eternal, life-directing, fragile, indestructible, controversial, expensive dimension of your existence.[12]

Perhaps we sometimes ignore the soul because it is so mysterious. We can't see it or touch it. We can't take its pulse or check its blood pressure. How can we know when the soul is bruised or injured or malnourished?

I think we realize our soul is in desperate need of attention when we act like that old Wurlitzer piano. We look good on the outside, but the inner workings of our life are out of tune. We paste a smile on our face at work, but we don't feel any joy. We nod in agreement while our kids are talking, but we're not actually listening. We go through the motions of singing hymns and following along with the Sunday sermon, but our hearts are far from worship.

That's when you need to "pay close attention to yourself." That's when it's time go to the Soul Spa for spiritual renewal.

The good news is that God is able to take our out-of-tune lives and bring them back into harmony. That old piano that hadn't been tuned in ten-plus years seemed hopeless, but we decided to take a chance on it. We found a master piano technician who painstakingly tuned every string. Then came back a month later to do it again. Finally, he was able to bring the instrument back to its original function—making beautiful music.

When we meet with our heavenly Father, He is able to take every discordant note in our lives and make them ring true once again. He will take our yearnings, our emptiness, our apathy and transform them. He is able to make our soul sing.

Too often we place our value in our appearance, our success, and our accomplishments. We polish the outside. But we forget that our true value is in who we are inside—a redeemed child of God. We strive for recognition, for power, for romantic love but ignore our original purpose—bringing praise to a gracious, generous, and glorious God.

Paul told Timothy, "Pay close attention to yourself and to your teaching; *persevere* in these things" (1 Timothy 4:16 NASB, emphasis mine). We kept that old Wurlitzer for three years but it took perseverance to keep it in tune. Even after the two major tunings, we couldn't expect it to stay in tune. Every six to twelve months, we hired a professional to get the inside working as well as the outside. We, too, must exercise perseverance in our soul care. We must come to the Master Technician often to allow Him to erase the effects of living in the world and bring our spirits back into harmony with Him.

I pray that our forty-day journey of spiritual renewal will be an opportunity for an extensive soul adjustment. I hope these pages will provide the tools to *keep* your heart in tune with your loving, gracious heavenly Father.

The Holy Spirit is ready to meet you each day at the Soul Spa to restore your soul.

Holy Spirit, I admit that I sometimes neglect the most important part of my being—my soul. I come to You today for inner healing and renewal. Take my weariness, my emptiness, my apathy and transform them. Tune my heart to sing Your praise. In Jesus' name. Amen.

Soul Study

1. That old Wurlitzer piano looked good on the outside but had been neglected on the inside. How would you describe the current state of your soul and your care of it? Check any that apply.

    _____I regularly take time to care for my soul.

    _____I rarely think about paying attention to my spirit.

    _____People looking at my life would probably think I pretty much had it all together, but inside I feel like I'm falling apart.

    _____Right now, a few strings are out of tune, but my heart is fairly well-aligned with Christ.

    _____I love God, but I feel my life is too hectic for regular soul care.

    _____I want to find more time to meet with God for soul upkeep.

2. Read the following verses and write down what God does for our souls.

    a. Psalm 19:7

    b. Psalm 25:20

    c. Psalm 94:19

    d. Psalm 107:9

    e. Matthew 11:29

3. Which of the verses above addresses the current state of your soul (question 1)? Turn the words of that scripture into a prayer asking God for His gentle soul care.

4. Write out this week's memory verse.

Group Activities

1. For your first meeting, give your group participants a taste of a luxury spa. Use some of these ideas to create a spa atmosphere.

   Dim the lights and place lighted candles around the room. (Consider electronic candles if your meeting place doesn't allow an open flame.)

   Play relaxing music in the background—think slow classical music or soft jazz.

   Bring in a small electronic waterfall for the soothing sound of water.

   Buy some fragrant flowers and place them in small vases around the room.

   Set out some fresh fruit and small, scrumptious chocolates.

   Invite the participants to arrive in their fluffiest robes.

   Give small favors shaped like flip-flops with this week's memory verse attached.

2. Discuss the week's readings and Soul Studies. Allow each woman to choose one question that speaks to her heart. After she gives her answer, open up that question to the other members of the group. The leader may highlight other concepts and questions.

3. Invite everyone to gather for a time to come into God's presence. Use some of the ideas in the Spa Session (page 15) to create an awareness of God's nearness.

4. Close in prayer.

STUDY: DELVE INTO SCRIPTURE

Spa Food

A relaxing spa experience includes healthy, delicious food that tantalizes your taste buds and nourishes your body. You might find yourself feasting on grilled salmon and strawberry meringue pie or ricotta lasagna and a chocolate soufflé. Spa chefs take great pride in preparing delectable treats that are surprisingly healthy.

Christ has also prepared a feast for us in Scripture. His words nourish our spirits and refresh our souls. As we absorb each bit of God's Word, it goes deep into our hearts and changes them.

> It is not that you will think about what you have read, but you will feed upon what you have read. Out of a love for the Lord you exert your will to hold your mind quiet before him. In this peaceful state, swallow what you have tasted . . . take in what is there as nourishment.[13]
>
> Jeanne Guyon

MEMORY VERSE

Your words were found, and I ate them,
and Your words became to me a joy.
Jeremiah 15:16a

A MODEL OF STUDY

*After three days they found Him in the temple,
sitting among the teachers, listening to them and
asking them questions. And all who heard Him were
amazed at His understanding and His answers.*
Luke 2:46—47

The temple. As Levi walked through the Court of the Gentiles, he marveled at the marble walls towering fifteen stories above his head. He was on his way to meet other teachers of the Law to discuss the Torah. Walking past the booths set up to sell sacrificial animals, he heard pigeon coos. A lamb bleated. As Levi turned to look at it, he bumped into someone.

"Levi, dear friend, watch where you are going!"

Levi looked back to see that he was face-to-face with one of the other teachers. "Ehud, so sorry! I'm just on my way to our usual spot. Has anyone arrived yet to take up our discussions?"

"Yes, there is quite a group there today. In fact, a young man has joined our conversations and has amazed everyone with His knowledge of Scripture! Go on ahead, they are over there." Ehud pointed to a spot under the colonnades. "I will join you later. I must take care of some business."

Levi found the spot between the stone columns and took an empty seat. His friends were engaged in a lively conversation. He was surprised to see that the newcomer Ehud had mentioned was a boy of only twelve or thirteen. Yet He asked insightful questions and answered Levi's colleagues' queries with amazing wisdom for one of such a young age.

Levi leaned over to Jacob and asked, "Who is this young man? Is this Thomas's grandson?"

Jacob whispered in Levi's ear, "No, we are not sure who He belongs to. He says His name is Yeshua. He's been here for three days. His knowledge of Scripture is amazing."

Just then a worried couple approached the little group. When the woman saw the young man, she ran up to Him and flung her arms around His shoulders. "Yeshua, thanks be to God! We were so worried! Have You been here the whole time?" But then, she pulled away and lowered her voice, "Son, why have You treated us like this? Your father and I have been anxiously searching for You!"

"Why were you searching?" the young man answered. "Didn't you know I had to be in My Father's house?"

It was obvious that the parents didn't have a clue of what He meant by that. And . . . neither did Rabbi Levi.

Jesus modeled the discipline of study for us. As true God, He had no need to study Scripture with the teachers of the Law in the temple. But in His love for us, He set aside His divine nature and humbled Himself to study His own Holy Book.

Yet Jesus went to the temple to study with these learned men. He had a three-day conversation about Scripture. What can we learn about the Spiritual discipline of study by observing Jesus' example?

Study takes time. Jesus spent three days in the temple with the teachers, listening, conversing, and asking questions. In-depth study takes time.

We all have busy lives. With families and jobs and laundry and car pools, three days devoted to Scripture study sounds like an impossibility. But what if we all periodically took an extended period of time to delve into God's Word? What if we carved out an afternoon to go to a library, a park, or a retreat center to go deep into Scripture?

Study needs to be a priority. To Jesus, talking with the teachers was more important than going home with the group from Nazareth. By waiting those extra three days, He missed out on playing with His friends on the way back home. How often do I choose study over entertainment? Not very often.

Study is a natural response to being a child of God. Jesus' explanation to His parents was "Did you not know that I must be in My Father's house?" (Luke 2:49). He understood the need to be in the temple talking with others who loved God's Word.

When we love someone, we want to know more about them. We find out what they've done in the past and we try to discover their hopes and dreams for the future. We, in effect, study them. And when we like what we know about them, we want to know even more. The more we know about our Father's love and grace and goodness, the more we want to know. Study becomes a natural response.

Study involves listening. Luke's account tells us Jesus was sitting among the teachers, listening to them. If we are going to learn anything, we will need to listen.

We can study by listening to great teachers like Jesus did. Paying close attention to your pastor's sermon on Sunday is a great place to start. We can also "listen" to great teachers by reading books about God's Word. Commentaries, Bible study books, and devotionals are all ways to learn more about Scripture and how to apply it to your life.

But most important, we need to listen to the Holy Spirit as we read God's Word. Study doesn't mean reading the Bible just so we can check off "devotions" on our to-do list. It means opening God's Word and expecting the Holy Spirit to reveal a surprising facet of God's love or teach a refreshing truth. It means watching for a holy nudge to act on what we've read.

Study involves asking questions. Luke 2:46 says Jesus was "sitting among the teachers . . . and asking them questions." Of course, Jesus knew all the answers, but He was modeling an important facet of study—curiosity.

As I read and study Scripture, I'm always asking questions. We will learn more about asking questions this week, but the most important question is "God, what truth or lesson do You want me to see in this passage today?" Whether I'm studying a specific book of the Bible or following a read-through-the-Bible-in-a-year plan or preparing for my ladies' Bible study group, I'm listening for the Spirit's prompting: *Pay attention to this. This is what you need today.*

Study of God's Word is the foundation of our Spiritual practices. Scripture is how God speaks to us. When we neglect Bible study, our spirits become parched. We thirst for God. But our Lord longs to quench our thirst by speaking His words of peace, love, and forgiveness to our souls.

The more we hunger for God's Word, the more we will be satisfied. Study God's Word and be filled.

Father in heaven, thank You for the gift of Your Word. As I open my Bible, help me to clearly hear Your voice. Give me a hunger for the spiritual food available in Scripture. Satisfy my thirsty soul. In Jesus' name. Amen.

Day One

Soul Study

1. When we are really hungry, we grab and eat almost anything, from a healthy apple to a bag of barbecue potato chips. Describe how you feel when you've made the healthy choice versus the quick but not-so-nourishing snack.

2. When our stomachs are hungry, they growl. What are some of your symptoms when your soul is hungry?

3. What are some of the things you do to feed your soul?

4. Read Luke 2:41–52.

   a. Jesus spent three days talking with the teachers in the temple. Study of Scripture takes time. Write about the time you spend in Scripture study. Some questions to consider: When do you study the Word? How often? Do you want more time to study? Where could you find more time?

   b. Jesus chose staying behind to discuss theology with some old men rather than going home with his family and friends. How do you make Scripture study a priority?

c. Jesus listened to the teachers in the temple. What is one thing you can do to listen to the Holy Spirit as He teaches you in the Word?

d. Jesus modeled curiosity—He asked questions. Ask yourself this question today: Lord, what truth do You want me to see in Luke 2:41–52 today? Write down the most important lesson you learned from this passage.

5. Write out this week's memory verse.

Spa Session

Sometime this week, find a morning or afternoon or even an hour to get away from your usual routine to go deep into Scripture. Get away to a park or coffee shop and ask the Holy Spirit to help you see Christ more clearly in the Word.

Some suggestions for this time:

☼ Color-code Psalm 19. Use colored pencils to highlight themes. For instance, color the terms for God's Word in red, the phrases that tell what God does for you in yellow, and what our part is in blue. Meditate on the how these colors intertwine and what this means in your life.

☼ Read a short book of the Bible, like Philippians or Colossians, three times. Keep a notebook nearby and write down key words and themes. You might even want to outline the lessons of the book. Ask the Holy Spirit what lesson is most important for your life today.

☼ Listen to a psalm. Get an audio version of the Bible or click to listen on BibleGateway.com. Close your eyes and picture the imagery the psalmist uses. Some psalms to try: Psalm 1; 23; 27; 31; and 42.

☼ Take a walk outside. Before you go, read a Gospel story and print out a copy of it to put in your pocket. As you walk, imagine yourself as a character in the story and picture all the sights, sounds, and feelings that person would have experienced. Some Scriptures to try: Luke 7:11–17; Luke 10:25–37; and Luke 10:38–42.

Write about your experience here or in a journal.

Day Two

BIBLE STUDY

They said to each other, "Did not our hearts burn
within us while He talked to us on the road,
while He opened to us the Scriptures?"
Luke 24:32

I'm a Bible nerd. There, I've said it.

I admit I've always been a bit of a nerd. I was the student who actually studied in study hall. I was the kid who liked algebra class more than phys ed. I have always loved to learn, and learning about the Bible is no exception.

When I was thirteen or fourteen, my mother gave me a Living Bible. Before opening that Bible, I had been struggling through a King James Version. I was constantly tripped up by all the *thees* and *thous* and the archaic language.

But when I read the Living Bible, the words made sense. A whole new feast of learning opened up. I sensed God speaking to me in His Holy Word as I read in bed every night before I went to sleep.

During my high school years, a new course in the feast of Scripture came through a study offered by a Bible teacher trained in Greek. Some of my high school friends (fellow Bible nerds) and I attended the class on Colossians, and we slowly devoured this book bite by bite, carefully pondering each verse. Now, I was not only inspired by the Bible, I was discovering deeper meanings and truths that changed my life.

Somewhere along the way in my Bible study feast, I noticed there were themes in the Bible. Love was talked about often. Peace was mentioned a lot. Joy was a frequent topic. I began a notebook where I listed a topic at the top of a page, and every time I found a verse on that subject, I wrote down the reference. I thought I really had something useful—until someone told me you could buy a book like that. It was called a concordance.

The discovery of the concordance led me to do many topical studies of the Bible. I have notebooks filled with notes from my years of Bible study—a record of my feeding on the Word.

Because you are reading this book, I know that you, too, possess a strong desire to know Scripture better. Maybe this is your first Bible study, or maybe you've been a lifelong student of the Bible. Either way, I'm sure you'll agree there is always more we can learn about Scripture.

The Book of Luke tells a story about two men who enjoyed a feast on God's Word with the best Bible teacher possible—Jesus. Cleopas and his friend were walking from Jerusalem to the town of Emmaus after Jesus' death. While they were walking, another man joined them and talked with them about what had happened in Jerusalem the past few days. They were surprised when this man explained what the Scriptures had to say about Jesus' life and death and resurrection. But later, they were even more surprised to discover their Scripture tutor had been Jesus Himself.

When they reached Emmaus, they invited Jesus to stay and dine with them. But even before they ate the bread and drank the wine, they had been consuming the Word. They had a Scripture feast. What can we learn about enjoying our own Scripture feast from this story?

Yesterday we learned study involves asking the right questions. As we examine the principles of Scripture study in the Emmaus story, we will explore them in the form of questions you can use to prepare your own Scripture feast.

- **How does this passage teach me to walk more closely with Jesus?** The two disciples strolled with Jesus on the Emmaus road—He met them while they were on their way. The resurrected Lord promises the same to His present-day disciples. He accompanies us on His way; and He promises to meet us where He makes Himself available: His Word.

- **Holy Spirit, what does this passage mean?** As Jesus walked with the two disciples, He interpreted "in all the Scriptures the things concerning Himself" (Luke 24:27). On our own, we can't understand Scripture. We can only receive the Word as a gift and rely on the Holy Spirit to guide us in our study.

- **How can I use this passage in my life today?** When Jesus pretended to be going on farther, the two disciples urged Him to stay with them. It's easy to read the Bible as a daily assignment, check "morning devotions" off our to-do list, close the book, and go through our day without thinking any further about what we have read. But what if we were like Cleopas and his friend and asked Jesus to *stay* with us? Ask the Holy Spirit to show you how you can use what you have read in your activities today.

- **What action does this passage motivate me to take?** As soon as Jesus revealed Himself, the two disciples got up and immediately walked the seven miles back to Jerusalem. Jesus didn't command them to tell the other disciples of His appearance, but they couldn't keep the good news to themselves. When we study God's Word, the Holy Spirit will inspire us to take action.

Asking these kinds of questions will help us to enjoy a daily Scripture feast—a feast that will nourish our starving souls and quench the thirst of our spirits. As the Word goes deep inside us, it changes us from the inside out.

Cleopas and his friend noticed this change. After Jesus left them, they said, "Did not our hearts burn within us while He talked to us on the road, while He opened to us the Scriptures?" (Luke 24:32). Something unmistakably real happened in their hearts when Jesus spoke. When God speaks to us through His Word, our hearts are stirred. Our passion for Jesus is rekindled.

We are fed. We are moved. We are transformed.

Jesus, my soul aches to know You more. Meet me in Your Word. As I read, please open up the Scriptures to me. Enable me to understand the meaning and the action I need to take. Make Your Words real in my heart. Amen.

Soul Study

1. I'm a self-described Bible nerd. How would you describe your own experience in Bible study?

   a. I'm a New Testament Newbie.

   b. I'm a Gospel Groupie.

   c. I'm a Scripture Student.

   d. I'm an All-in Apprentice.

2. The Emmaus disciples said, "Did not our hearts burn within us while He talked to us on the road, while He opened to us the Scriptures?" (Luke 24:32). Describe your experience when the Holy Spirit makes Scripture clear to you.

3. Asking the right questions will help us get more out of Scripture study. Use the questions we gleaned from the story of the disciples on the road to Emmaus to study Matthew 5:1–16.

   a. How does this passage teach me to walk more closely with Jesus?

b. Holy Spirit, what does this passage mean?

c. How can I use this passage in my daily life today?

d. What action does this passage motivate me to take?

4. Lord, what truth do You want me to see today?

5. Write out this week's memory verse.

Day Three

SCRIPTURE MEDITATION

My soul will be satisfied as with fat and rich food, and my mouth will praise You with joyful lips, when I remember You upon my bed, and meditate on You in the watches of the night.
Psalm 63:5—6

Meditating on Scripture. What a lovely thought.

However, even though I love reading Scripture, studying Scripture, and discussing Scripture, *meditating* on Scripture is not easy for me.

It seems whenever I decide to reflect on a favorite Bible passage, it doesn't take long for my mind to jump from Ephesians or Colossians or Proverbs to *Didn't I just hear the dryer buzz? I should take care of the laundry. Remember to make that dentist appointment. Spring break is coming—should we try to get away? DON'T FORGET TO BUY TOILET PAPER. There goes the dryer again.*

Can you relate?

Somehow when I'm rushing around running errands or doing chores, sitting down in a comfy chair and meditating on God's Word sounds simply delightful. But when I finally get to that chair and relax with my Bible on my lap, my thoughts bounce around in my brain like clothes in a dryer.

Many times my attempts to meditate end up in frustration and guilt. *Why can't I make my mind behave? Why can't I focus on something for just ten minutes?* Meditation seems so mysterious. *Just sitting and thinking—how does that work?* Meditation sounds so pious. *Can an ordinary Christian like me actually do it?* Meditation can even seem scary. *Is meditation all about emptying the mind, like I've heard?*

Indeed, not all types of meditation are helpful. Eastern meditation, which emphasizes clearing the mind and disengaging from the world, can be dangerous. Jesus warned an empty mind may be an invitation for evil to take up residence there (Luke 11:24–26).

But Christian meditation is different. Instead of trying to empty the mind, Christian meditation focuses on filling the heart. Rather than disengaging from the world, meditating Christians aim to connect with Christ. And the best way to do this is to meditate on God's Word.

John Kleinig writes in *Grace Upon Grace*, "Christian meditation focuses on Christ and His Word. It starts with Jesus and ends with Him. His Word empowers our meditation and determines what happens in it. His Word brings life and light, comfort and health to the soul."[14]

Meditating on God's Word is a feast for the soul. Psalm 63:5–6 says:

> My soul will be satisfied as with fat and rich food,
> and my mouth will praise You with joyful lips,
> when I remember You upon my bed,
> and meditate on You in the watches of the night.

Meditating on Scripture is like enjoying a rich delicacy. Picture yourself at an elegant spa, sitting down to a delicious meal. Every course dances on your taste buds. Last but not least, dessert comes—a delicate chocolate mousse. You take one bite and let the chocolate slowly melt on your tongue. You spoon tiny amounts out of the goblet to make it last longer, savoring every bite.

That is what meditation can be. Savoring each morsel of God's Word. Consuming it in tiny portions. Letting the meaning go deep into your soul.

When I think of meditation in this way, I do it out of love, not guilt. I appreciate the privilege of an intimate relationship with Christ. I still struggle with those bouncing thoughts, but I try to accept God's grace and allow Him to teach me to better focus on Him without berating myself.

Here are a couple of Scripture meditation methods I find helpful.

Meditating on Bible stories. Use your imagination to put yourself in a Bible story. Picture yourself as the woman healed of a twelve-year hemorrhage or as a mother of one of the children Jesus blessed. Read a Gospel story and ask the Spirit to guide your thoughts. See the scene in your mind. What sounds do you hear? What scents are in the air? Use all five senses to put yourself there.

Martin Luther recommended that when you read a Gospel story and you see Christ interacting with someone, imagine you are there with Him.

When you see how he works, however, and he helps everyone to whom he comes or who is brought to him, then rest assured that faith is accomplishing this in you and that he is offering your soul exactly the same sort of help and favor through the Gospels. . . . Christ is yours, presented to you as a gift.[15]

Remember, Jesus is the same yesterday and today. Through the Gospel stories, He produces trust in us. Believe He is able to give you the same help and grace that He gave people two thousand years ago.

Meditating on scriptural imagery. Jesus told stories. Paul used word pictures. David's psalms are full of metaphors and symbols. Almost every chapter of the Bible uses imagery. As we meditate on those images—pictures from the seen world to depict the unseen world—the Holy Spirit can lead us to a fuller understanding of God.

One of my favorite images in the psalms is in Psalm 119:162: "I rejoice at Your word like one who finds great spoil." I picture someone who has just discovered a treasure chest in a cave. He pulls it out into the light and opens the lid. It's full of jewels—emeralds, diamonds, and rubies—all sparkling in the sunshine. He jumps to his feet and dances around. His joy is overflowing at finding a true treasure.

Then I think about how God's Word is that for me—a treasure chest full of priceless gems. Each truth is another facet of God's love for me. My imaginings take me to different emotions: Contrition that I often act as if material possessions are more valuable than this spiritual fortune. Sadness that not everyone in the world has his or her own copy of this treasure. Joy and thankfulness that God would give me such wealth.

Meditating on God's Word is not about completely understanding Bible history or translating every Greek word correctly. It's not about achieving a perfectly quiet mind or avoiding all distracting thoughts.

Meditation is hearing the Spirit's voice and letting Scripture come alive in our hearts. It's feasting on every morsel and letting it go deep into our souls. As we feed on God's Word, it nourishes our spirits and transforms our minds.

Holy Spirit, help me listen to Your voice in Scripture. Make each word come alive. May the richness of the Word nourish my heart and transform my spirit. In Jesus' name. Amen.

Day Three

Soul Study

1. Write down three words that come to mind when you see the word *meditation*.

2. Reread Psalm 63:4–5. Does thinking about Scripture meditation as a satisfying feast change your views of meditation? How?

3. Try one of the meditation methods mentioned in today's reading. Write down any insights you gained during this time.
   Suggestions:
   • Meditating on a Bible story: Matthew 14:22–33; Luke 8:40–48; or John 5:1–15.

- Meditation on scriptural imagery: Psalm 23; Luke 8:4–15; 1 Corinthians 9:24–27; or Ephesians 6:10–18.

4. Lord, what truth do You want me to see today?

5. Write out this week's memory verse.

Day Four

SCRIPTURE MEMORIZATION

Lay up these words of Mine
in your heart and in your soul.
Deuteronomy 11:18

I am a keeper of memories.

I try not to save a lot of "stuff." I regularly purge my clothes and shoes. I actually like to clean out my closets. My clutter-busting operations can get so intense, my husband will joke that he's glad he is not out on the curb.

But the stuff of memories I save. (I hang on to my hubby too!) We have scads of scrapbooks. Dozens of picture albums. Thousands of digital pictures on our computers.

Because I want to remember. I want to relive the day I said "I do" to that wonderful husband. I want to recall the impish look on my son's face when he pushed an ice-cream cone on my nose at his first birthday party. I don't want to forget my daughter's lopsided smile when she was missing a front tooth.

It turns out God wants us to remember too. In fact, the word *remember* appears over 150 times in the Bible.[16] Our Lord wants us to recall His words to us. Deuteronomy 11:18 says:

Lay up these words of Mine in your heart and in your soul.

Perhaps when you think of Scripture memorization, you think of your days in Sunday School or Vacation Bible School. You diligently memorized the required verses so you could get a gold star or a cool prize. But probably as soon as Sunday School or VBS was over, you promptly forgot those Scriptures.

I know that's what happened to me. I think it was because I fixed the words in my mind, but not in my heart.

God does not want us to memorize His Word as an intellectual exercise only. Yes, any kind of memorization requires concentration and repetition. But if we are only memorizing the words and not the message, the words won't go deep into our souls.

Another section in the Book of Deuteronomy gives us detailed instructions on how we can internalize God's Word:

> Hear, O Israel: The LORD our God, the LORD is one. You shall love the Lord your God with all your heart and with all your soul and with all your might. And these words that I command you today shall be on your heart. You shall teach them diligently to your children, and shall talk of them when you sit in your house, and when you walk by the way, and when you lie down, and when you rise. You shall bind them as a sign on your hand, and they shall be as frontlets between your eyes. You shall write them on the doorposts of your house and on your gates. Deuteronomy 6:4–9

Memorize Scripture out of love. This section of Deuteronomy begins with the command to love the Lord with all our heart, soul, and strength. Moses then immediately gives the children of Israel instructions on how to learn and recall God's Word. Why? Because when we love someone, we hang on his or her every word. We cherish love letters and mushy cards. It isn't a chore to remember what our loved ones have said to us; it's a joy. God wants us to store up His Words for the same reason I want to stockpile pictures—out of love.

Keep God's Word in your *heart.* In school, we often had to memorize things like vocabulary words or calculus equations. We crammed facts into our minds to pass the test and, if we didn't need the information afterward, we quickly forgot them. It was merely an intellectual exercise.

While any kind of memorizing requires the intellect, memorizing the Bible is primarily training for the heart. Scripture in our heart refashions the fibers of our soul, changes our attitudes, and refocuses our wills. Storing God's Word in our mind *only* is like storing it in a data file on your computer. It can be accessed and reviewed, but it doesn't change the computer. But when we internalize God's Word in our heart, it's a bit like those daily computer updates, rewriting the code of our operating systems.

Make Scripture memory a part of your everyday life. Moses instructed the Israelites to talk about God's Word when they were sitting at home and when they were out on a walk. It was a part of their daily routines.

When we hold a stockpile of Scripture in our hearts, we can mull over John 15:5 while we're cooking a meal or walking the dog. We can recite verses with our children at mealtimes and talk about the meaning at bedtime.

Nighttime has become an especially powerful time for me to review God's Word. Somehow, when I lay my head on my pillow, I immediately think of all the stupid things I did that day. Or all my to-do-list anxieties resurface. Even after I have prayed, confessed, and turned my worries over to God, my mind will run over the concerns like a hamster on an exercise wheel.

But recently, I started using memorized Scripture as my new hamster wheel. I am able to get off the wheel of regret and worry and hop on the wheel of God's Word. I review His words of love. And as I run over these verses again and again, God gives me peace, contentment, and . . . sleep.

Make Scripture visual. Moses told God's people to tie Scripture symbols on their hands and write them on the doorposts of their homes. We can do the same. Using Scripture art on our walls helps us to remember God's Word and is a witness to those who visit. Post the verses you are memorizing on your refrigerator, mirror, or computer wallpaper.

Internalizing God's Word is like eating healthy food at a spa. The food is full of nutrients that fuel our bodies and bring healing to every cell. As we slowly take in God's Word, it brings health to our soul. As we fix God's Word in our mind and our heart, it changes us. The words, woven into the fiber of our soul, transform our attitudes and emotions.

I have heard it said that when we memorize Scripture, we allow the Holy Spirit to speak to us in His own language. Storing God's Word in our heart lets the Spirit pull up words of hope to us whenever we are discouraged. He is able to use God's commands as a warning to keep us out of trouble. And He can whisper reminders of God's love when we are hurt, ridiculed, or even downright depressed.

Be a keeper of the Word.

Lord, I want to be a keeper of the Word. Help my mind and heart store up Your Word. Use these words to caution me when I'm headed for danger. Remind me of Your promises when I'm disappointed. Help me to remember Your words of love. Amen.

PRACTICAL TIPS FOR MEMORIZING SCRIPTURE

☼ *Choose verses that are meaningful to you.* When a verse speaks to your heart, you are much more likely to remember it. You will pull it out of your memory bank whenever you need encouragement or peace.

☼ *Write the verse on a card you post by your computer or sink.* Review it while you are waiting for the computer to boot up or while you are washing dishes.

☼ *Recite the verse or verses you are memorizing* while you are walking, doing chores, or—as I do—when you are trying to go to sleep.

☼ *Use technology.* Try the Bible Memory app (http://www.remem.me) to put your memory verses on your phone or tablet. This app gives you ways to learn and review the verse and then put it into a cycle to periodically review. Or use the Scripture Typer website (http://scripturetyper.com) or Bible Minded (http://biblemindedapp.com), which has memorization plans, different memorization methods, and ways to track your progress.

Day Four

Soul Study

1. I'm a keeper of memories—I save photographs. What do you save or collect? Why?

2. Today we learned storing God's Word in our hearts is like rewriting the code of our operating systems. How have you found this to be true?

3. Look up these verses and write down the benefits of keeping Scripture in our hearts.

   a. Psalm 37:31

   b. Psalm 40:8

   c. Psalm 119:11

   d. Isaiah 51:7

4. Lord, what truth do You want me to see today?

5. Write out this week's memory verse. Use one or more of the Scripture memorization tips to help you put the verse in your heart.

SACRED READING

Oh how I love Your law!
It is my meditation all the day.
Psalm 119:97

My now-husband John and I spent the year we were engaged going to two different schools five hundred miles apart. I was finishing a music education degree in Eau Claire, Wisconsin, and John was starting his seminary education in St. Louis.

Now, this is going to date me, but this was before we even had access to text messages, cell phones, or email. Even long distance phone calls were rare because they were so expensive. So we wrote letters. Yep. We used paper and pen, envelopes and stamps.

Because we were in love and yet so far apart, I treasured those letters. I would read and reread them. I was living in a house with three other music students where it was difficult to find quiet time alone, so sometimes I ducked into the closet under the staircase to the second floor for a little privacy. I cherished John's words.

Did you ever think of reading the Bible that way? Too often I read it like a school assignment. Or like a set of instructions. Or as a dry and dusty history book.

Yet God's Word is truly His love letter to us. The Bible is full of His words of affection, His affirmations of devotion, and His declarations of love. When we read and reread about His passion for us, we cannot help but love Him more.

Recently, I discovered a way to read Scripture that helps me read it more like a love letter. This method will not help you read through the Bible in a year or obtain a chronological view of biblical events (both good things, by the way), but it will help you listen to God's voice in Scripture. As you use this SACRED reading process, you will read God's Word like an intimate letter. You will cherish the words because they are the words of the One who loves you.

SACRED reading uses times of reading and times of prayer—times of talking and times of listening. To use this method, you will choose a short passage of Scripture—about six to eight verses. Follow these steps using the word SACRED to remind you of the process.

Silence your thoughts. Begin by quieting your spirit. Call on the name of the triune God and ask the Holy Spirit to guide your time of listening. Perhaps pray Psalm 119:18, "Open my eyes, that I may behold wondrous things out of Your law" or 1 Samuel 3:9, "Speak, LORD, for Your servant hears."

Wait silently on the Lord. At first, your thoughts may seem to crowd out any quietness, but let them pass through your mind as if you are watching a parade move down the street. Bring your thoughts back to your loving Father and eventually the cacophony in your head will die down.

Attend to the passage. Read your chosen verses. Ideally, you will read the passage out loud. While studying the psalms in Hebrew, Luther "discovered that all the Hebrew words for the practice of meditation referred to various forms of vocalization and sub-vocalization, ranging from speaking to murmuring, chattering to musing, singing to humming, muttering to groaning."[17] In Hebrew, meditation involved actually using your voice.

Read slowly. Pause when it seems that God is drawing your attention to a particular sentence or phrase. Let the words resonate in your heart.

Contemplate the Word. Meditate on the passage, especially on any words the Holy Spirit seems to be speaking directly to you today. Ask yourself questions like "What do I experience as I read this text: resistance? joy? peace?" "Do these words inspire thanksgiving or contrition?" "How is this passage speaking to my life?"

Do not hurry this time. Let the Holy Spirit speak to your heart. Allow Him to bring up any feelings, doubts, or fears buried deep in the recesses of your soul. Thoroughly explore your soul for your most genuine response to these words of God.

Respond to the text. After you have taken time to listen, speak. That is, pray, pouring out your heart to God in response to what He has just spoken to you. If the passage inspired joy, offer thanks. If it brought a sense of conviction, confess. Spill out any fear, doubt, anger, or frustration. Be totally honest with God. He invites you to a deeply personal dialogue with Him.

Exhale and rest. Read the text again and rest in the love of God. Acknowledge His presence with you right now, and receive His peace. Simply wait with the Lord who loves you more than you can know. Relax in the arms of God.

Dwell in the Word. As you come out of this restful state, ask the Spirit, "What truth can I carry into my day?" Think about a truth or promise you received that will help you live out God's Word. During the day, reflect on what the Holy Spirit spoke to you in your SACRED reading.

My connection to God has grown deeper as I have practiced this SACRED reading. At times, God speaks words of comfort to my battered soul. Other times, He brings me to my knees as He reveals my pride or sense of entitlement. His words may inspire a boundless joy that spills out in praise or arouse a repentance that trickles out in tears.

I'm learning to open my heart to God and express my true emotions, even if they are not pretty. I figure that if David could do it in the psalms, God must not mind. As we empty out the chaos and confusion, He can replace the tangled feelings with His comfort, His forgiveness, and His love.

Read God's love letter to you. Pore over His words and let them sink deep into your soul. Treasure His words of grace.

Dearest Lord, thank You. Thank You for writing a rich and precious love letter to me that I can read every day. I cherish Your words of grace. Help me to hear You speak to my heart whenever I open Your Word. Amen.

Day Five

Soul Study

1. Which word below best describes your view of the Bible?

_____textbook

_____instruction manual

_____love letter

Why do you see it that way?

2. Try the SACRED reading process described on pages 58–59. Read 1 John 4:7–12 and follow the prompts below. After you finish, write down anything you want to remember from this time.

Silence your thoughts. (Allow your mind to quiet down.)

Attend to the passage. (Read the passage out loud, pausing when the Spirit brings a part of it to your attention.)

Contemplate the Word. (Meditate on the passage, asking, "How does this passage speak to my life?")

Respond to the text. (Pray, pouring out your heart to God in response to what you have read.)

Exhale and rest. (Read the text again and simply rest in the love of God.)

Dwell in the Word. (Take a truth or promise with you into your day.)

3. Lord, what truth do You want me to see today?

4. Write out this week's memory verse.

Group Activities

1. Eat some spa food. Prepare something healthy and delicious. Search for spa food recipes on the Internet or try this one:

SPICY BANANA COOKIES

> ¾ c. all-purpose flour
> ¾ c. whole wheat flour
> ¾ tsp. baking soda
> ¼ tsp. salt
> 2 tsp. ground ginger
> ¼ tsp. ground cinnamon
> ⅛ tsp. ground cloves
> 1 banana, peeled
> ¾ c. granulated fructose* or granulated sugar
> 1 egg, slightly beaten
> 3 tbsp. molasses
>
> *Fructose is available in most health food stores

Preheat oven to 350°. Cover baking sheets with parchment paper or grease lightly. In medium bowl, combine flours, baking soda, salt, and spices. Mash banana in large bowl. Blend in fructose, egg, and molasses. Mix in flour mixture. Spoon tablespoons of dough 2 inches apart, onto prepared baking sheets. Bake 10–12 minutes or until golden brown. Remove to wire racks to cool completely.

Yield: 4½ Dozen. Per serving (2 cookies). Calories: 53, Fat: 0 g (5% calories from fat), Protein: 1 g, Carbohydrate: 12 g, Cholesterol: 7 mg, Sodium: 61 mg[18]

2. Discuss the week's readings and Soul Studies. Allow each woman to choose one question that speaks to her heart. After she gives her answer, open up that question to the other members of the group.

3. Talk about the Spa Session activities. Ask: Which activity did you choose? What was your experience with it?

4. Participate in a time of SACRED reading together. Sit together, but silently read and meditate on Isaiah 43:1–7. Follow the prompts on page 60. After fifteen minutes of silent reflection, divide into groups of two or three, and talk about the experience.

5. Come back together as a large group to close in prayer.

OPEN: EXPOSE THE HEART

Spa Treatments

Part of the spa experience is to simply get away from the routine of life. The spa surrounds you with people who pamper you—if only for a little while. Part of the pampering comes in the form of special spa treatments.

Some of these treatments are designed to purify your skin. Facials, body wraps, and saunas get rid of unhealthy toxins. As your skin opens its pores to shed impurities and dirt, the result is a smoother, cleaner surface.

This week at the Soul Spa, we will explore several treatments that will help us open our hearts to the Holy Spirit so He can do His cleansing work. We will learn how solitude and silence can renew our souls and open our hearts to our deepest longings. The Spiritual practice of examen is a treatment designed to let God's presence heal our wounded souls. And we will see how spiritual journaling can allow the Holy Spirit to uncover emotions we try to hide—even from ourselves.

> When Thou dost knock at my heart's door, let me not keep Thee standing without but welcome Thee with joy and thanksgiving.[19]
>
> John Baillie

MEMORY VERSE

He said to them, "Come with Me by yourselves to a quiet place and get some rest."
Mark 6:31 NIV

Day One

A QUIET PLACE

And rising very early in the morning,
while it was still dark, He departed and
went out to a desolate place, and there He prayed.
Mark 1:35

Where was Jesus? I couldn't understand it. After the exhausting day we had yesterday, I was sure He would still be sleeping. Yet clearly the Teacher was up and already out of the house.

The day before had begun with Jesus teaching in the synagogue and dramatically healing a man possessed by an evil spirit. The people of Capernaum were amazed at His teaching and His authority over demons.

After Jesus answered many questions, I managed to get Him away from the crowds by inviting Him to my home to rest. But even at home, there was no time to relax. My wife met Jesus at the door with a furrowed brow. Her mother was sick with a fever. Could Jesus please help?

Jesus placed a kind hand on her shoulder. "Lead the way," He said. We walked to the back room of the house where my mother-in-law tossed and turned on her bed. The Teacher went to her, took her hand, and pulled her to her feet. Instantly, the fever was gone. In fact, my mother-in-law insisted we all sit down while she prepared the evening meal.

But Jesus didn't rest long. People heard about the healing of the man with the evil spirit; by evening, it seemed the whole town was at our door.

I was about to go outside to tell them to go home. Jesus needed rest. But Jesus went to the door and slowly walked through the crowd, gently touching the sick and injured. Cries of joy erupted in little pockets of those gathered as people got up off their mats or threw down their crutches.

It was very late by the time everyone went home. Even Jesus' eyelids were beginning to hang heavy. We all lay down and slept.

But now it was breakfast time and Jesus wasn't here. Where could He have gone? How could He have had the energy to get up so early?

"Perhaps you should go find Him," my wife urged. "Make sure every-thing is all right."

I grabbed Andrew, James, and John. We pulled on our cloaks against the morning chill and greeted the few people already on their way to the market.

"Have you seen Jesus?" I asked. By now, the whole town knew the great Teacher and Healer, but most had not seen Him this morning.

We walked through the city, looking down every alley and side street until there were no more streets. No Jesus. Finally, Andrew spotted a figure in the distance, all alone in a field. As we neared, we realized it was our Teacher. He was kneeling by a rock, head lifted to the sky.

"Jesus! Everyone is looking for You," I exclaimed, then immediately wished I hadn't interrupted Him. He had so few moments to Himself.

Bracing against the rock, Jesus pushed Himself to His feet. He smiled at us and said, "Then let's go! We'll head out to some other villages and preach there too. After all, that's why I have come!"

Silence and solitude. We tend to avoid these things. Our society rushes from one activity to the next, afraid to slow down long enough to be labeled as boring.

But Jesus seemed to crave solitude and silence. In his Gospel, Mark tells us Jesus "went out to a desolate place" (Mark 1:35). In fact, Jesus often went off by Himself to spend time with His Father.

When I have read the stories of Jesus seeking time alone with His Father, I used to think He probably did it as an example for us. After all, He was God. He was in constant communication with His Father. He didn't need to be in a synagogue or the temple or the wilderness to hear His Father's voice. He had stored up the Word in His heart.

But as I read this story from Mark again, I think Jesus truly felt a compulsion to go to a place where He could be alone with His Father—just the two of them. No one pulling on Him to go to a sick relative. No one asking questions. No one clamoring for His attention.

Think about it. After the previous draining day Jesus had experienced, you would assume what He required most was sleep! I would have pulled the blinds shut, put a pillow over my head, and tried to sleep late into the morning. Instead, Jesus got up before the sun peeked over the horizon and went to a place where He could be alone.

Having an intimate time with the Father energized Him in a way sleep couldn't. A space in the schedule for just the two of them renewed His body and spirit more than eight hours of rest could. When the disciples found Him, He was ready to go. The time of solitude had revitalized His strength and refocused His purpose.

One rejuvenating aspect of a spa is the quiet. Voices are hushed. Music is muted. Our brains recover from the noise of the world. This week, we will explore how we can use the disciplines of silence and solitude to recharge our spiritual batteries and open our hearts to God. The clutter of our lives seems to block our view of Christ. Time alone with God will help us to see Him at work in the tangle of our activities. Journaling our thoughts can help unlock our souls, making room for the Holy Spirit to speak to us.

It is in solitude we can be real with God. In silence, we can hear His voice.

Father, my life is busy and chaotic and messy. I long for time to be alone with You. Teach me to make space in my life for solitude and silence, that I may hear Your voice more clearly. Open my heart to your healing touch. In Jesus' name. Amen.

Day One

Soul Study

1. Spa treatments, such as facials and saunas, are designed to help our bodies rid themselves of impurities. Have you experienced those spa treatments? Or if you haven't experienced them, how do you purify your skin? Describe the feeling when your skin is extra clean.

2. Write your reaction to this statement from our reading today: The clutter of our lives seems to block our view of Christ.

3. Read Mark 1:21–39.

    a. Jesus had a hectic day. In each box on the left-hand side of the chart below, write one event of that day. For example, in the first box, you could write: Jesus taught in the synagogue.

Events of Jesus' Hectic Day	My Natural Reaction

b. Next, picture yourself, experiencing the same day. Of course, Jesus was God and could do things we cannot do, such as heal people. But He was human too. He got hungry and tired just like we do. If you were experiencing the same day, what would be your natural reactions to the events Jesus experienced? For example, I love teaching, so being able to teach in the synagogue would have energized me.

c. After a day like that, what would you have done the next morning?

d. What did Jesus do (v. 35)?

e. Reread verses 37–38. What did Jesus' time alone with the Father seem to do for Him?

f. What does time alone with God do for you?

4. Lord, what truth do You want me to see today?

5. Write out this week's memory verse.

Spa Session

This week, we explore activities that open our hearts to the Holy Spirit's cleansing work. Find some extra time this week to try one of these:

☼ **Spend time with God through music.** Listen to hymns or praise songs, letting the music wash over you. Concentrate on the words. What is God whispering to you through the lyrics?

☼ **Sit where you have a view of nature.** If the weather allows, go to a park. If not, sit at a window with a view of creation. Consider the gift of God's beautiful world. Thank Him for His display of might and creativity.

☼ **Journal.** Writing down your thoughts often helps to unscramble them. Pour out your heart to God. Be totally honest and open. If you are afraid someone might read those candid words, destroy the pages when you are done, accepting God's grace. (For some journal prompts, look at page 90.)

☼ **Wash your face.** Martin Luther wrote, "When you wash your face, remember your Baptism." This week, as we focus on spa services, such as facials, make a point of recalling God's cleansing work in salvation. Write Luther's words on a sticky note and put it on your bathroom mirror. Buy yourself a new bar of pretty facial soap or a spa-like facial scrub. Every time you wash your face this week, remember your position as a redeemed, baptized daughter of God.

Day Two

SOLITUDE

And behold, the Lord *passed by, and a great and strong wind tore the mountains and broke in pieces the rocks before the* Lord, *but the* Lord *was not in the wind. And after the wind an earthquake, but the* Lord *was not in the earthquake. And after the earthquake a fire, but the* Lord *was not in the fire. And after the fire the sound of a low whisper.*
1 Kings 19:11–12

When I was a young mom, the thing I craved more than anything was a little time alone.

An introvert at heart, I draw energy from time to myself. But in the days of babies and toddlers, time alone was rare. The baby cried to be fed. The toddler pulled on my pant leg impatiently waiting for me to play.

One day, when the kids were both engrossed in an episode of *Sesame Street*, I thought I could at least sneak into the bathroom by myself. Maybe I'd have two minutes alone. But thirty seconds after I closed the door, I heard a little tap-tap.

"Who's there?" I called out (knowing full well it was the two-year-old).

A little voice from the other side of the door peeped, "It's me—cutie pie!"

Solitude can be an elusive thing. People surround us at our workplaces, in our homes, and in our churches. And we need people. We were created for community.

But at times, we need solitude—time alone to concentrate on only one Person.

The world constantly demands our attention. Sometimes the only time we can truly hear God is when we shut out all the other voices. We need solitude to hear the Father's whispers to our hearts.

The prophet Elijah experienced a time of burnout and depression after a very successful time of ministry. In response to his ragged feelings, he took a forty-day journey to Horeb, the mount of God. He instinctively knew he needed time alone with the Lord. Elijah's journey to solitude in 1 Kings 19 can help us with our path to hearing God in the empty places of our souls.

In solitude, we can sort out our feelings. When Elijah first arrived at Mount Horeb, God asked him, "What are you doing here, Elijah?" (1 Kings 19:9). God, of course, knew everything that was going on in Elijah's scrambled feelings, but I love that He asked Elijah that question. He knew it would help Elijah to put words to his emotions.

Sometimes, it takes getting away by ourselves to actually notice what is going on inside our messy hearts. When we find time alone with God, He asks us, "What are you doing here? What problems do you need to lay down? What soul hurts need to be healed?" In solitude, we can bring our empty souls to God and allow Him to speak His Word into them.

Elijah doesn't try to make his answer sound spiritual. He doesn't try to cover his raw feelings with a fancy wrapping of theological jargon. He tells the Lord:

> I have been very jealous for the LORD, the God of hosts. For the people of Israel have forsaken Your covenant, thrown down Your altars, and killed Your prophets with the sword, and I, even I only, am left, and they seek my life, to take it away. 1 Kings 19:10

Elijah shows us we can truly open our hearts to God. We can pour out the fear, the anxiety, even the self-pity. And God will listen.

In solitude, we can more clearly hear God's voice. After Elijah poured out his feelings, God told him to "go out and stand on the mount before the LORD" (1 Kings 19:11). The Lord was about to grace Elijah with His presence. A strong wind tore through the mountains, an earthquake shook the hills, and a fire swept past, but God wasn't in any of those.

Finally, there was a gentle whisper—and it was the voice of God.

We would have no problem hearing Him if God always spoke with the drama of a tornado, earthquake, or fiery inferno. But He often speaks in a gentle whisper, and the cacophony of our busy lives and the crescendo of our stressful days threaten to drown it out. Solitude helps us listen.

In solitude, we experience the miracle of God's grace. What did God say in that gentle whisper? He asked again, "What are you doing here, Elijah?"

After Elijah met God on the mountain, I expected him to give a profound answer like, "I'm here to meet with You, O Most High God. I'm here to see Your power."

But instead, Elijah gives the very same answer he gave before. The very same! Once again he talks up his zealousness for God, whines about the other people who have left the faith, and voices his fears for his life.

Let me tell you, I was extremely disappointed with Elijah. I wanted proof here in 1 Kings that time alone with God transforms a person. And even though Elijah had experienced a powerful wind, the quaking earth, the fire, and the soft whisper of God's voice—he hadn't changed a bit.

Maybe what is even more surprising is that God doesn't reprimand Elijah. He doesn't scold the prophet for whining. Instead, God gives Elijah strength in the form of practical instructions. The prophet is to anoint a helper prophet and some new rulers to help him in his fight against idolatry. God lets Elijah know that seven thousand in Israel have not yet bowed to Baal. Elijah is not as alone as he thought.

God cared enough about Elijah to give him practical answers to his problems. Even though Elijah's heart may not have been transformed by God's dramatic display of power and intimacy, God gave Elijah what he needed at that moment. He provided support.

Although I wanted this passage to demonstrate that solitude changes us, I think it shows an even more important truth: God's grace meets us where we are. He gives us what we need in the moment, whether it is a sense of peace, a renewed trust, or practical instructions for our daily lives.

God lets us come to Him as a whiny, griping mess. His grace is available to us even if we don't immediately shape up. He is patient with us even when we fail to demonstrate trust in His power.

The Father invites us to solitude so we can hear His whisper above the noise of the world. He asks us to come away with Him so we can pour out the messy contents of our hearts. He beckons us to time alone so He can give us what we need.

Holy Father, help me to hear Your quiet voice in the midst of my noisy world. I am grateful that You are willing to meet me right where I am and that Your grace is available even when I may be a grumbling mess. Thank You for always providing exactly what I need. In Jesus' name. Amen.

Soul Study

1. Some people are naturally invigorated by solitude and silence. Others find their energy with people. What about you? Do you lean more toward finding renewal in solitude? Or in people? Mark where you find energy on the line below.

I find energy
and renewal
in solitude.

I find energy and
renewal in being
with people.

2. Read 1 Kings 19:1–18.

    a. In verses 4–7, Elijah is in the wilderness—already alone. Why do you think he takes a forty-day journey to lonely Mount Horeb (v. 8)?

    b. When Elijah reached Mount Horeb, God asked him, "What are you doing here, Elijah?" (v. 9). If God asked you that question right now, what would your answer be?

    c. God asked Elijah the same question after He displayed His power, might, and tenderness in the earthquake, fire, and gentle whisper. Imagine yourself at the mouth of the cave, hearing God's gentle whisper, "What are you doing here?" Would your answer change?

d. How does God's answer to Elijah in verses 15–18 comfort you?

3. Lord, what truth do You want me to see today?

4. Write out this week's memory verse.

Day Three

SILENCE

For God alone my soul waits in silence;
from Him comes my salvation.
Psalm 62:1

One of my grandsons is particularly talkative. An incredibly energetic four-year-old, he is constantly on the move—cooking in his play kitchen, pushing his Thomas trains around a track—all the while making up imaginative stories and scenarios. My daughter tells us they never wonder where Andrew is, because they can always hear him.

One day, Andrew told his mother, "You know Mom, I don't know how to do silent."

So true. True for Andrew and true for many of us. We simply don't know how to do silent.

Silence is hard to find. Our world is a noisy place. In the office, copiers are thumping and phones are ringing. At home, silence is broken by children crying and microwaves beeping. Even when we look for quietness, it seems impossible to obtain.

Silence can be uncomfortable. We don't know what to do in the quiet. It seems empty, and so we fill it with music, talk, or activity.

Silence can be scary. When the noise of the world is stilled, we can hear our own deep doubts and fears. We try to drown our insecurities, anger, and loneliness in an ocean of busyness. But in the quiet, long-suppressed longings, sadness, and exhaustion can bubble to the surface.

Although silence can be uncomfortable, scary, and hard to find, it is also where we are better able to hear God speak. In the hush, we can slip into God's alternate universe for a little while. In the quiet, it's a bit easier to see from an eternal perspective.

Psalm 62 is a beautiful treatise on silence. The opening words of King David demonstrate he was a student of stillness:

> For God alone my soul waits in silence; from Him comes my
> salvation. Psalm 62:1

David knew that silence helps us shut out our noisy, clamoring distractions and realize what is always true: God is with us. But sometimes we have to wait in the quiet and still our souls to sense His presence. Too often I view my devotion time like a trip to a fast-food restaurant. Stop in for a minute. Get some nourishment. Get on with my day. I expect God to speak *now*. Often He does. But if I waited a little longer in the silence, would I hear Him a little better? Would He have more to say if I stayed in the quiet a few more minutes?

David goes on to say,

> He alone is my rock and my salvation, my fortress; I shall not be
> greatly shaken. Psalm 62:2

In the silence, I better hear God's reminders that my salvation, my protection, and my peace come only from Him. In the stillness, I realize all I possess is from my Father. In the quiet, I remember there is nothing I can do that will make God love me more.

David ends the psalm with a reminder that God speaks to us. In the quiet, we are able to hear His voice.

> Once God has spoken; twice have I heard this: that power
> belongs to God, and that to You, O Lord, belongs steadfast love.
> Psalm 62:11–12a

In the silence, God told David about His character. In fact, God repeated Himself and twice told David about His power and His love. When we still our hearts, God reminds us to rest in His unfailing love and let Him take care of the challenges of the day. Once when I was in a particularly busy season of life, I decided to try an experiment. I was afraid my tendency to get absorbed in my work would result in an all too familiar state—heart-strangling stress. I wondered what would happen if, during this hectic time, I purposely took small snatches of time to focus on God and His awesome love for me.

While I was working at my computer, I set a timer for thirty minutes. When the timer rang, I quit what I was doing and closed my eyes. For just a minute or two, I turned my thoughts to God. I reminded myself of His incredible love for me.

The difference in my work week was astounding. My productivity was not diminished by taking these minibreaks, and I was able to complete my tasks without the usual anxiety and stress. Basking in God's love for just a few moments reminded me to work in His strength.

Try using silence to connect with God in a deeper way. Today, use one of these suggestions for stillness.

Unplug. Try a media fast. For a set amount of time (say an hour or two), unplug from your computer, tablet, phone, and TV. Tell yourself, no email, podcasts, or Pandora. Take a walk or do some chores in silence. Notice what a time of quiet does for your soul.

Wait. Sit in a quiet place. Set a timer for ten minutes. Repeat David's words, "For God alone my soul waits in silence." Tell God, "I'm here," and wait. Let the silence open your heart to what is hiding inside. Are you feeling sad, angry, lonely, or exhausted? Are there deep longings that you keep pushing down out of sight? Sit with your thoughts and emotions without trying to deny them, without trying to fix them. Give them to God and let Him do His work.

Stop. Use my experiment to find snatches of quiet in your day. Use a timer to remind yourself to stop every thirty or sixty minutes to take minibreaks of silence. Close your eyes and remind yourself God is with you in that moment. Repeat David's words, "Twice have I heard this: that power belongs to God, and that to You, O Lord, belongs steadfast love" (Psalm 62:11b–12a).

Silence is the steam bath that opens our heart to our deepest longings. In the quiet, the Holy Spirit may unlock emotions we try to hide, consciously or unconsciously. God's spa treatment of love allows our souls to come clean with honesty and transparency.

Heavenly Father, I come to You in silence. Help me to drown out the world's noise and listen to Your voice. Unlock any hidden thoughts and emotions. Open my heart to Your steadfast love. In Jesus' name. Amen.

Day Three

Soul Study

1. Which of these statements most resonates with you?

   Silence is hard to find.

   Silence is uncomfortable.

   Silence is scary.

   Why is that statement true for you?

2. Use the SACRED reading process as the Holy Spirit speaks to you through Psalm 62. Read the psalm and follow the prompts. After you finish, write down anything you want to remember from this time.

   Silence your thoughts. (Allow your mind to quiet down.)

   Attend to the passage. (Read the passage out loud, pausing when the Spirit brings a part of it to your attention.)

   Contemplate the Word. (Meditate on the passage, asking, "How does this passage speak to my life?")

   Respond to the text. (Pray, pouring out your heart to God in response to what you have read.)

   Exhale and rest. (Read the text again and simply rest in the love of God.)

   Dwell in the Word. (Take a truth or promise with you into your day.)

3. Try one of the three silence activities described in today's reading. Use the space below to record your reactions to the experience.

4. Lord, what truth do You want me to see today?

5. Write out this week's memory verse.

Day Four

EXAMEN

My presence will go with you,
and I will give you rest.
Exodus 33:14

It happened on an ordinary December day. I was driving down a busy street on my way to a meeting. I turned a corner and right there in my Chevy Impala, I felt God's presence. It was as if the whole car was filled with echoes of God whispering, "I love you." I was so overcome with the sense of God's nearness that my eyes filled with tears and I had a little trouble seeing the road. Who knew an ordinary sedan could be a place to meet the almighty God?

Of course, God is always with us. Hebrews 13:5 records God's promise to us, "I will never leave you nor forsake you." But I don't always *sense* His presence. And when I do, it is usually in a worship setting: singing a favorite hymn in church, listening to a praise song on the radio, or reading God's Word in my devotional time. Sometimes, during my hectic days, I forget that God is *always* near, not only when I am in church or reading my Bible.

The Spiritual discipline called examen is a tool we can use to discover God's nearness in our everyday lives. God is with us when we worship with fellow believers and when we sit down to read His Word, but He is also close when we are going to the grocery store, bathing our toddlers, and driving in our Chevys or Fords. We just don't always perceive Him.

Examen is a centuries-old practice of noticing where God shows up in ordinary moments of our day. It's a time of reflection that helps us contemplate God's nearness in the midst of our frenzied schedules and mundane chores. During this time of prayer and meditation, we look for God's nearness and assistance.

There are many ways to practice this Spiritual discipline, but here is a way I find helpful and inspiring.

Recognize God's presence. Begin by finding a quiet place. Relax and turn your thoughts to God. Remind yourself God is with you in this moment. Recite Hebrews 13:5, "I will never leave you nor forsake you." Pray these words back to God saying something like, "Thank You, God, that You are always with me, sheltering my fragile heart and propping up my worn and weary soul."

Review your day. Ask the Holy Spirit to guide your thoughts through this process. Close your eyes and go over the last twenty-four hours in your mind. Watch the day play out as if you are watching a movie of your life. Recognize your kind and merciful Father's hand throughout the day. Identify moments when you now wish for a retake. Push the pause button on these moments, and examine your feelings in those moments—good or bad.

Remember the words of Psalm 139:1–2:

> O LORD, You have searched me and known me! You know when I
> sit down and when I rise up; You discern my thoughts from afar.

Pray this psalm using words like "Loving Father, I know You saw all that happened in the past day. You are aware of all of my thoughts and feelings. You were present every minute. Help me to see the day through Your lens. Point out any places where I may have shut You out or fallen short. Make me aware of Your loving presence. Thank You for Your gifts of grace each day."

Respond to God's leading. Reexamine the moments where you paused the film of your day. Thank God for every moment you were mindful of His presence. Where you were at fault, ask for forgiveness. Recall Exodus 33:14:

> My presence will go with you, and I will give you rest.

Rest a moment in God's love and pray something like "Father, I thank You that You are always with me. Make me aware of Your Presence as I go through my day tomorrow. Give me the grace to love You and love others." Consider praying a hymn such as "O Holy Spirit, Grant Us Grace" or "Renew Me, O Eternal Light."

When I first began the practice of examen, I looked for more "Chevy Impala moments"—times when God's presence filled my heart. I expected the discipline to make moments when I *felt* close to God occur more often.

Disappointment set in when this didn't happen. But as I continued the discipline, I realized that while moments when I sense God's overwhelming presence may be rare, God shows His nearness in little pieces of every day. I notice Him in the sweet smell of a lilac bush I pass. I'm reminded of Christ's care in the smile of a friend. I detect Him in the protection I receive when a car comes dangerously close to mine, but misses.

For instance, yesterday was a day full of ordinary activities. I taught a few piano lessons, volunteered at a homeless shelter where I am tutoring a woman who is studying for her GED, and completed a few errands around town. During my examen time, I saw God in His gift of work—I love teaching piano. At my tutoring session, we ended with prayer, and the woman I tutor prayed a powerful prayer—God was definitely present in the basement of that homeless shelter! While I was running my errands, I was caught in a torrential rainstorm. At the time, I thought only about dodging puddles, but reviewing the day through God's lens showed me His presence in the opening of the heavens and the cleansing rain.

In the ritual of the examen, we open our hearts and minds to the searching of the Holy Spirit like a cleansing facial opens the pores of our skin. We shed the impurities of the day and invite God's healing presence into the pores of our life. He is already there. Examen enables us to notice Him in the ordinariness of our days. The more we practice examen, the more we find God in the unexpected. We see Him in His Word, but are also reminded of His presence in the stark beauty of one lone rose on a bush, the reassuring embrace of a friend, the rhythm of a soaking summer rain. God is near.

Holy Presence, forgive me when I forget You are always near. As I scurry through my days, help me to be aware of You in each moment of the day. Help me to see You in the touch of a friend, the beauty of Your creation, and the truth of Your Word. In Jesus' name. Amen.

EXAMEN YOUR HEART

Here are a few more questions you might find useful in your practice of examen.

☼ How was God with me today?

☼ When did I notice God guiding me? protecting me? helping me? prompting me?

☼ What parts of my day were life-giving?

☼ What parts of my day were life-draining?

☼ When did I feel the peace of God's nearness?

Day Four

Soul Study

1. Have you ever had a "Chevy Impala moment"—a time when you clearly felt God's presence? Write about the experience here.

2. Read Exodus 33:12–23.
   a. What were Moses' three requests (vv. 13, 15, 18)?

b. What might your life look like if you prayed those three prayers every day?

c. What is God's promise in verse 14?

d. How does God do that?

e. What part of God did Moses see (v. 19)? What part of God did Moses not see (v. 20)?

f. We also may not always see direct evidence of God, but He often demonstrates His goodness. What signs of God's goodness have you seen lately?

3. Try the spiritual practice of examen. There is no set time to do this discipline. I have done it in the morning, reviewing the previous day and recording the evidence of God's presence in my journal. I have also done it at the end of the day when I lay my head down at night, and I find it a peaceful way to close the day and fall asleep. Follow the steps outlined on page 83. Journal about your experience here.

Recognize God's presence.

Review your day.

Respond to God's leading.

4. Lord, what truth do You want me to see today?

5. Write out this week's memory verse.

Day Five

JOURNALING

These things I remember, as I pour out my soul.
Psalm 42:4a

God, where are You? You feel so far away. I need Your presence—here, now, with me. Where can I go to feel You near?

I've been crying my eyes out, every day, every night. I'm pouring out my soul to You. Do You hear?

But I keep telling myself, "Don't lose hope. God will come through." Lord, I know that, in the end, You will work everything out. So even here in the dark times, I will praise You.

What if the author of Psalm 42 were writing today? What if you could peek into his twenty-first-century journal? Would his words sound something like those above?

The whole Book of Psalms feels like an incredibly personal journal—a beautiful, poetic diary. But even in the beauty, we see an outpouring of raw emotion and desperate feelings. David and the other psalmists didn't hold anything back when they wrote the 150 songs we find in the middle of the Bible. They wrote out of both joy and depression. They expressed trust and doubt. They recorded their ecstatic hopes and their deepest fears.

Our own spiritual journals may not be read three thousand years from now, but they can be a place to empty out the cupboards of our hearts. Blank pages invite us to pour out our souls with complete honesty and transparency. As we write, we can bring all of our dreams and aspirations, all of our anxieties and misgivings, all of our frustrations and disappointments to the feet of God.

I have kept a spiritual journal for years. For me, it isn't a place to chronicle the events of the day. Instead, I use the pages to keep a record of the Scripture passages I read and the lessons God teaches me through His Word. Writing untangles my confused and intertwined thoughts. Journaling helps me work through problems. Like a mud bath at the spa refines my skin, journaling distills my thoughts.

Maybe you have never kept a spiritual journal before. Perhaps you tried in the past, but the practice grew stale. Maybe you journal regularly, but you want to go deeper. Let's use the example of Psalm 42 as a way to keep a spiritual journal.

Begin with God. The psalmist begins writing his journal entry by seeking God. He writes, "When shall I come and appear before God?" (v. 2b). The goal of a spiritual journal is not to write perfect prose or to meticulously record the events of every day. The purpose of a spiritual journal is to draw closer to God. As you begin writing in your spiritual journal, ask the Holy Spirit to guide your thoughts and sort out your words.

Express your emotions. The author of Psalm 42 tells God about the tears he sheds every day (v. 3) and talks about his turmoil (v. 5). He freely pours out his soul.

Because a journal is private, it can be a safe place to dump out our frustrations, disappointments, hurts, fears, doubts, and grief. We can bring them all to God through the prayers of our pens. We don't have to hold anything back, thinking our thoughts aren't spiritual enough. God knows our hearts anyway. He wants us to open up to Him so He can mend our tattered feelings.

Explore what is behind the emotions. The psalmist asks himself a question, "Why are you cast down, O my soul, and why are you in turmoil within me?" (v. 5). After you have emptied out your heart and named your emotions, ask yourself, "Why am I feeling this way?" Ask the Holy Spirit to help you discover the cause of your feelings. Perhaps you will find a spiritual reason behind some negative emotions, such as the need to believe God's words of grace to you or the necessity to forgive someone in your life. Or you may uncover a purely practical cause of your pent-up frustrations: your body demanding more rest or your soul requiring time with a friend.

In one recent journal entry, I was pouring out my weariness at my never-ending to-do list. I complained that I felt that there was always more to accomplish and never enough time to do it all. As I was writing, I decided to make a list of all the things I felt I had to do. When I looked at the finished list, I realized many of the items were things no one was holding me responsible for. I simply felt I "should" do them. This was making my list of activities and chores unreasonably long. It was impossible to complete them all.

Put your hope in God. In Psalm 42, the psalmist reminds his soul to "hope in God; for I shall again praise Him, my salvation and my God" (vv. 5b–6a). On our own, we can't make sense of our emotions. But when we turn to God, He can shine His light on our dark feelings. After writing my list and reading God's Word, I recalled Jesus' words "Come to Me, all who labor and are heavy laden, and I will give you rest" (Matthew 11:28). Perhaps this kind of rest would be possible if instead of composing an impossibly long to-do list every day, I simply asked my heavenly Father to reveal the *one* thing He wanted me to do. Perhaps then I would remember that joy that lasts doesn't come from checking off an item on my to-do list, but from resting in God's presence. Without my journal, I may not have realized that my felt burden of responsibilities was a weight I placed on myself. It was one God was willing to take and remake.

As you journal, ask the Holy Spirit to direct you to a Scripture that speaks to your problem. The psalmist wrote, "My soul is cast down within me; therefore I remember You" (v. 6)—remember what God has done for you in the past. Reflect on God's love for you—"By day the LORD commands His steadfast love, and at night His song is with me" (v. 8). Then, thinking of God's loving, faithful character, write down what He might say to your heart in this moment. What passages of His Word address your pain, your hurt, your disappointments? Trust His promises and remind your soul to hope in Him.

A spa promises to purify your skin through facials, saunas, and body wraps. You leave the experience rid of impurities. You are cleansed. Use the Spiritual practice of journaling to allow God to cleanse your soul. Pour out your feelings to the Father. Let Him untangle the jumbled mess of your emotions. He is our hope.

Holy Spirit, thank You that You are always with me. Remind me of Your nearness as I pour out my soul. Help me to take the time to explore what is in my heart and what is behind my messy emotions. I know You can take the tangled mess of my soul and make it right. In Jesus' name. Amen.

Soul Study

1. Do you journal? Or did you keep a diary as a young girl? Describe your experiences with journaling or diary-keeping.

2. E. M. Forster wrote, "How can I tell what I think until I see what I say?" Write your reaction to this quote.

3. Read Psalm 42.

   a. This "journal entry" voices a range of emotions. Sometimes the psalmist expresses despair and sometimes hope. Write down phrases from the psalm that convey these feelings under the proper heading.

Despair	Hope

b. The psalmist expresses both positive and negative feelings. How does that help you in writing in your spiritual journal?

c. Try your hand at spiritual journaling. Write for ten minutes (or longer, if you wish). Answer these questions from Psalm 42 or simply pour out your soul. Ask God to guide your journaling time. Ask yourself, "What am I feeling?'

Ask the Holy Spirit, "What is behind these feelings?"

Remind yourself to hope in God. Find a verse that deals with your feelings or remind yourself of God's help in the past. What do you think God is saying to your heart now?

4. Lord, what truth do You want me to see today?

5. Write out this week's memory verse.

Group Activities

1. Have a spa day with your group and try a facial together. Buy a prepared facial mask or do an Internet search for homemade facial masks. This yogurt-oatmeal mask promises to clean out your pores.

YOGURT-OATMEAL FACIAL MASK

3 tbsp. oatmeal
2 tbsp. yogurt

1 tbsp. olive oil
1 tbsp. lemon juice

Grind the oatmeal in a food processor until very fine.
Add yogurt, olive oil, and lemon juice. Blend.

To use:
Wash face with mild soap and warm water.
Rub the oatmeal mask on your face.
Let it sit for 10–12 minutes.
Wash it off with lukewarm water.
End with a cold-water rinse to close your pores.
Don't forget to take pictures of your facial experience!

(Alternatively, if you do not want the mess of the home facial, open up a discussion about personal cleansing regimens. Give everyone an opportunity to share how they take care of their skin. Share what works and what doesn't!)

2. Discuss the week's readings and Soul Studies. Allow each woman to choose one question that speaks to her heart. After she gives her answer, open up that question to the other members of the group. Ask some of the women to share their experience with the Spa Session activities from page 69.

3. Participate in examen together. Each woman will follow the prompts on page 83 to silently open her heart to God's presence. After fifteen minutes, divide into groups of two or three, and talk about the experience.

4. Close in prayer.

UPLIFT: WORSHIP THE LORD

Spirituality

At the spa, rough skin can be smoothed and muscles can be relaxed. But many spas do not limit their services to the body. Elite spas may also provide spiritual counselors who strive to soothe troubled minds and souls. As more and more people are rejecting traditional religion, spas have become a place to seek out spirituality. Spas are marketing themselves as temples of wellness.[20]

Spa staffs include spiritual counselors, intuitives, and energy readers who want to guide you on a path of self-discovery, help you listen to the inner self, and discover what your soul needs right now. Spa menus include classes on mind-body wellness, spiritual solutions, and healing the heart. People are using these services because they realize they are more than skin and bone. We all possess a spiritual side as well.

Fortunately, we do not have to rely on human spiritual counselors or New Age practices to nourish our spirits. The almighty God of the universe is reaching out to embrace our souls. The everlasting Father wants to feed our hungry hearts. As we visit the Soul Spa, we receive spiritual food from God's Word.

When we realize this, our spirits respond in worship. We lift up God's holy name. We praise His grace, His majesty, and His power. The Spirit lifts our hearts, and we raise up God's holy name. When we mindfully worship, we are focused on God and not on ourselves. His love and grace overwhelm our souls.

Lift up your heart, lift up your voice; Rejoice, again I say, rejoice![21]
Charles Wesley

MEMORY VERSE

Sing to God, sing praises to His name; lift up a song to Him who rides through the deserts; His name is the Lord; exult before Him! Psalm 68:4

A HOLY NIGHT

Father, the hour has come; glorify Your Son
that the Son may glorify You. John 17:1

It was Passover time. I had always loved this feast—a time to remember how the hand of God rescued His people from the oppression of Pharaoh. But this year would be even more wonderful because those of us who had followed Jesus for three years would observe this most holy day with the Son of God. I anticipated the celebration with joy.

Jesus gave Peter and John the mission to make all the preparations in Jerusalem, telling them exactly where they would find a room for our feast. When evening arrived, the rest of us entered and took our places on the floor around the long table. It was clear that I was not the only one who had anticipated this special meal. Before we began eating, Jesus looked around the table at all of us and said, "I have been looking forward to eating this Passover meal with all of you."

We had the usual elements of this sacred meal. Bitter herbs, charoset, a roasted lamb were all on the table. And we had not forgotten unleavened bread.

During the meal, Jesus stopped for a moment and took some of that bread and blessed it. He broke it and gave it to us. Then He said, "Take and eat, this is My body." Thomas passed me a piece of the bread, whispering, "What does He mean? This is His body?"

Then Jesus took the chalice of wine before Him, lifted His eyes, and gave thanks to God. He passed the cup around and instructed us to drink. "This is My blood of the covenant," He said. "It is poured out for the forgiveness of sins." Thomas's eyebrows knit in confusion as he passed me the cup. I certainly didn't understand the mysterious words either.

Jesus looked around the room at our confused faces. "Don't be troubled," He reassured us. "You believe in God, now trust Me. I am going to get a place ready for you. Trust Me in this: when the time is right, I will take you there with Me. We will eat and drink together in My kingdom."

As Jesus went on to teach us, I had the feeling these were His most important words to us. I sensed both a heaviness and a holiness in the room.

After a long pause, Jesus looked up to heaven and prayed. I felt as if we were listening in on a very personal conversation between a Son and His Father. We eavesdropped in awed silence. When He finished, we heard only the sound of our hearts beating. Someone started singing a hymn. We worshiped in song and went out into the night.

Imagine what it might have been like to have a seat at the Last Supper. Even as they praised the Most Holy God and remembered His care in the past, the disciples witnessed the institution of a new way of worship.

This week, we will study Spiritual disciplines related to worship—practices that lift up our almighty God. Looking at Jesus' celebration of the Passover, we can learn some principles of worship.

Worship glorifies God. Jesus began His High Priestly Prayer that night with the words, "Father, the hour has come; glorify Your Son that the Son may glorify You" (John 17:1). As an obedient Son, Jesus glorified the Father. The word *glorify* means to "cause the dignity and worth of some person to become manifest and acknowledged."[22] When we worship, we praise the Trinity. We give God the honor He deserves. We declare His majesty and worth.

Worship celebrates God and His gifts. That holy night when Jesus instituted the Lord's Supper, He and the disciples were celebrating the Passover, one of the seven feasts the Israelites were to observe. It was a night of joyous remembrance, recalling God's act of rescuing His people from Egyptian slavery. In fact, most of the feasts were exuberant occasions commemorating God's care in the past and praising His present blessings. As God's people, we are not to live dreary, dismal lives. Because our cup overflows with eternal blessings, we come together to worship the Great Provider in joy and thanksgiving.

Worship remembers Christ and His sacrifice. Jesus instituted His Holy Meal with the words "Do this in remembrance of Me" (Luke 22:19). It is only through Christ's blood that we hold the right to come into God's presence. We cannot even approach God without Jesus' sacrifice. In worship, we receive the true Lamb of God.

Worship reserves time for God. In celebrating the Passover, Jesus and the disciples followed God's instruction for setting aside time for worship. In addition to the seven yearly feasts the Israelites were to observe, they set aside one day a week to rest, spend time with family, and focus on the gifts their Holy God gave to them. In our rushing modern-day world, we tend to focus on doing and not receiving from our gracious giver, God. We have lost the art of Sabbath.

This week, we will examine how we can lift up the holy name of God. We will see how we receive God's grace, love, and strength when we approach Him in worship.

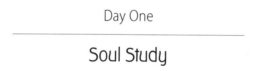

Holy God, I worship Your majesty. I praise Your power and strength. I am amazed at Your compassion and love. Yet I know my worship sometimes falls flat. May Your Holy Spirit guide me to a place of wonder and awe. Help me to accept Your gifts and receive them with joy. Amen.

Day One

Soul Study

1. How would you describe worship to someone who doesn't know God yet?

2. John 17 records the prayer Jesus prayed during the Passover celebration with His disciples. Read verses 20–26 using the SACRED reading process we discovered in Week 2.

Silence your thoughts. (Allow your mind to quiet down.)

Attend to the passage. (Read the passage out loud, pausing when the Spirit brings a part of it to your attention.)

Contemplate the Word. (Meditate on the passage, asking, "How does this passage speak to my life?")

Respond to the text. (Pray, pouring out your heart to God in response to what you have read.)

Exhale and rest. (Read the text again and simply rest in the love of God.)

Dwell in the Word. (Take a truth or promise with you into your day.)

3. Lord, what truth do You want me to see today?

4. Write out this week's memory verse.

Spa Session

Expand your worship experience this week. Reserve some time to glorify God and celebrate His gifts to you. Try a new worship practice. Here are some ideas.

☼ **Worship in song.** Create a worship playlist of your favorite praise songs on your digital music player or phone. Choose songs that turn your heart to God. Listen to this playlist while you're reading the Bible, walking around the neighborhood, or even scrubbing the bathroom. Worship along with the music.

✺ **Sing a hymn.** Memorize the words to a few timeless hymns, such as "Great Is Thy Faithfulness" or "Beautiful Savior." Pray these words back to the Father. Meditate on them while you're waiting in line or stuck in traffic.

✺ **Study a painting** that shows God's power, such as Michelangelo's "Creation of Man," or a painting of people worshiping, like Hubert and Jan van Eyck's "Adoration of the Lamb." Find the painting online, and take time to study it. What feelings does the painting evoke? How does it inspire you to worship?

✺ **Try a new worship posture.** Stand and raise your hands in adoration. Kneel by your chair in humble worship. Lie prostrate on the floor in awe. Repeat the words of the angels' worship chorus, "Holy, holy, holy, is the Lord God Almighty, who was and is and is to come!" (Revelation 4:8).

✺ **Read one of the worship prayers in the Bible.** Try Exodus 15:1–18; 2 Samuel 22:1–51; or Psalm 145. Rewrite the prayer in your own words, adding in your own reasons to praise God. Then, read it out loud to worship the Almighty.

Day Two

WORSHIP

God is spirit, and those who worship Him
must worship in spirit and truth.
John 4:24

Hawaii was on my bucket list. In fact, visiting each of the fifty states was on my bucket list. By 2010, I had checked off forty-nine of them. But Hawaii was still a dream—a far-off dream.

Then, in 2012, we heard about an amazing deal on a condo on the island of Kauai. Anyone who knows me well knows that my husband and I cannot resist a good deal, so we booked a trip to Hawaii.

We arrived on Kauai late in the evening. By the time we got the rental car at the airport and drove to the condo (the one of the fabulous deal), it was dark. As we unloaded our bags, we could hear the waves of the Pacific lapping the shore, but we couldn't see the ocean. We couldn't tell how close we were to the beach. Exhausted from the day's travel, we dumped our suitcases on the floor of the condo and tumbled into bed.

We woke up early. Too early. Our bodies were still on Central Time and, even though I was still tired, I couldn't get back to sleep. I got out of bed and shuffled into the living room and began to pull back the curtains.

Suddenly, I was wide awake. "John, come quick! And bring the camera!" I shouted back to the bedroom.

The vast Pacific Ocean was right outside our window! Due to our fondness for bargains, we had never had a room with an ocean view before. And at the very moment I peeked past the curtains, the orange sun was peeking out from a gray sea, slowly making its way into a pink and purple sky.

We quickly pulled on some clothes and ran the fifty feet to the beach to fully experience God's display of beauty. As we stood awestruck at the brightening sky, our hearts swelled in worship and we burst out in a chorus of "10,000 Reasons." The sun was coming up, a new day was dawning, and

God's majesty was evident. We had ten thousand reasons to praise the Immortal Creator.

Worship. Worship is our response to God's glory and grace reaching into our lives. When we truly encounter God, our hearts swell in worship. That's what happened to me when I saw the exhibition of God's majesty in Kauai. That's what happened when the Israelites in Nehemiah's day heard the Word of the Lord read after a long spiritual drought (Nehemiah 8). That's what happened when the exiled apostle John saw a vision of the almighty God (Revelation 1:17).

Yet my worship often falls flat. Sometimes when I praise God with my brothers and sisters in Christ, I'm not paying attention to the divine invitation to receive God's grace. My mind wanders to my grocery list, next week's appointments, and speculation on where the lady in front of me got that cute dress.

Jesus said, "The hour is coming, and is now here, when the true worshipers will worship the Father in spirit and truth, for the Father is seeking such people to worship Him. God is spirit, and those who worship Him must worship in spirit and truth" (John 4:23–24).

What does it mean to worship in spirit and in truth? I'm pretty sure it isn't the mindless activity I am sometimes guilty of on Sunday morning. And I don't think true worship prescribes a certain type of music or liturgy. Worshiping in spirit and in truth has more to do with our hearts.

The word "spirit" in John 4:23 can mean either the Holy Spirit, the spiritual element of our beings, or "the influence which fills and governs the soul."[23] To worship in Spirit is to respond to the Holy Spirit's presence inside of us, receiving both the grace and the ability to sincerely worship. It's pulling our hearts and minds out of a spiritual slumber to bow to the beauty of Christ. It's opening the curtain of hearts to God's influence so we cannot help but cry, "Holy, holy, holy."

The Greek word Jesus used for truth is *aletheia*. This word also has a couple of meanings. It can mean what is true in an objective sense—what is true no matter how you look at it. For instance, the moon is always orbiting the earth, even when we can't see it on a cloudy night. God is always mighty, always good, and always loving, even when current circumstances make us want to think otherwise. We are to worship God's character—His holiness, omniscience, beauty, and mercy—because that is always true.

Aletheia can also mean what is true subjectively—a sincere and genuine character, a "mind which is free from affection, pretense, simulation, falsehood, deceit."[24] We are to truly worship, not just go through the motions. To worship in truth is to actually mean what is coming out of our mouths, to think about the words of the psalms, hymns, and spiritual songs we are reciting.

Here are some practices that aid us in worshiping in spirit and in truth:

Don't save it all for Sunday. Worship every day. During your devotional time, read a psalm of praise, sing a favorite hymn or worship song, or honor God for who He is. Be aware of God's presence with you during the day. Sprinkle words of praise and thanksgiving into every hour, every moment.

Spiritually prepare for Sunday worship. Read the week's prescribed Bible readings ahead of time (ask your pastor for the upcoming week's Scriptures). Reflect on the past week and confess any sins God brings to mind (perhaps practice an examen of the whole week).

Arrive at worship ten minutes early. Lift up your heart to God in adoration. Tune your spirit to hear Christ's words to you. Be aware that you are in God's house, and mindfully let go of personal agendas and concerns. Pray for the pastor and worship leaders.

We worship because of the treasures we have received from the Father. And as we worship in spirit and truth, our spirits are transformed. We are not purely physical beings. Even those who do not follow Christ may seek out spirituality at a spa because they realize they cannot deny their spirit. Spa-goers undergo therapies that release negative emotions. They practice mindfulness and inner awareness.

But worshiping the one true God does even more than make us mindful of our spiritual side. It puts us in touch with our Creator. He lifts our eyes to see beyond our physical existence. He lifts our hearts to His wonder and grace. He lifts our spirits to experience the holy immensity and puts everything else in perspective.

So respond to God's greatness. Burst out in song. Explode in praise. We have tens of thousands of reasons to worship our one true God.

Father, my heart is filled with awe at Your love for me. I am amazed at Your creativity and might displayed in creation. I praise Your holiness, Your goodness, Your power. In Jesus' name. Amen.

Day Two

Soul Study

1. Write about a time when your heart spontaneously burst out in worship to God.

2. Read John 4:19–26. This passage is part of the story of Jesus meeting the Samaritan woman at the well. This encounter was remarkable for several reasons: the Samaritans were despised by the Jews, a Jewish man would never speak to a woman in a public place, and the woman had not led a respectable life. Yet Jesus chose to teach *her* about true worship.

    a. In verses 19 and 20, the Samaritan woman brought up a disagreement about worship of her day. What was that issue?

    b. What is Jesus' response to this issue (v. 21)?

c. What does He say is the most important element of worship (vv. 23–24)?

d. What are some issues of worship that cause disagreement in our day?

e. How can we apply Jesus' words to those issues?

f. Using what you have learned in today's reading, express in your own words what it means to worship in spirit and in truth.

3. Lord, what truth do You want me to see today?

4. Write out this week's memory verse.

Day Three

THE LORD'S SUPPER

The Lord Jesus the same night in which He was betrayed took bread:
And when He had given thanks, He brake it, and said, Take, eat:
this is My body, which is broken for you: this do in remembrance of Me.
1 Corinthians 11:23—24 (KJV)

I remember sitting on the floor of a church camp as a teenager. Our youth group was participating in an informal worship service. We sang. We listened. We shared favorite Bible verses.

When it came time for Holy Communion, the pastor pulled out a loaf of bread instead of the communion wafers I was accustomed to. We each pulled off a small piece of the loaf and passed it on while the pastor spoke the words "Take and eat, this is Christ's body, broken for you."

Broken for you.

Somehow the actual tearing of the bread made Christ's sacrifice more real than ever before. His body was beaten, pierced, and crucified—for me.

Now, on most Sundays, you will find me at the piano at the front of the church playing a hymn or praise song while I watch the members of my congregation file forward and receive Christ's body and blood. For some of our members, the trip to the front of the church is not easy. The short journey requires the aid of a walker or a wheelchair. One young woman with fibromyalgia sometimes needs the steady arm of an usher to lean on. They come broken.

In reality, we all come to the Lord's Table broken. Sin fragments our souls. Pride shatters our wholeness. Failures damage our relationship with God. We all come burdened, discouraged, wounded, and crushed.

And so we arrive at the Table to be healed. Christ's body was broken so we could be made whole. Jesus was crucified that our sins could be forgiven and we could be united with the Father once again.

I don't like to admit I'm broken. My prideful nature resists this. I want to be seen as competent and capable, not weak and wounded. I'd rather not admit my need for forgiveness.

It's at those times I may enter God's house without actually meeting Him there. Even as we sing, listen, and pray, I am thinking about my schedule, my responsibilities, my "important" life. My mind is not engaged in worship. I hold out my hand for the thin, white wafer. I drink from the cup. But I don't remember what it took for me to receive this sacred offering. When I don't realize my need, I don't appreciate the gift.

I want to change this. I want to remember Christ's sacrifice. I want to participate in Holy Communion, fully engaging my heart. I am beginning to practice a more mindful approach to the Table.

Before going to church to receive the Lord's Supper, I sometimes read one of the accounts of Jesus instituting this meal (Matthew 26:26–29; Mark 14:22–25; Luke 22:14–20). I put myself in one of the seats at the table and try to imagine the emotions I would have experienced as I broke off a piece of bread and took a sip of wine. I remember that Jesus is offering me the same blessings that He offered His disciples.

At the worship service, I try to fully participate in the confession of sins. Prayerfully revisiting the past week, I ask the Holy Spirit to reveal where I missed the mark. My spirit longs to receive God's flowing grace. I rejoice in the pastor's words, "You are forgiven."

I approach the Lord's Table with a humble yet joyful heart. I hold the bread in my hand for a moment, remembering Christ's broken body. I smell the wine in the cup before I take a sip. I taste the liquid of mercy and feel forgiveness run down my throat.

It's good to come to the Table broken. It's necessary to confess our sins and acknowledge our neediness. Our sins could not be paid off with a little bail money or a few hours of community service. It took a broken body. It took the blood of a perfect Savior to redeem us.

This week, we are talking about how health resorts may promote spiritual wellness. At a modern-day spa, you might encounter mystical spirituality. Receiving Christ's body and blood in the bread and wine of Holy Communion is certainly mysterious. We cannot understand it. Yet it is very real. His broken body and His shed blood repair our souls.

Come to the Lord's Table broken. For it's there our sins are forgiven. It's there our fragmented souls are put back together again.

Precious Savior, how can I thank You for Your great sacrifice? Your body was beaten and broken for me. Your blood was poured out to redeem my soul. Thank You for the gift of Your body and blood in the celebration of Your Supper. Bread of Life, feed my ravenous soul. Nourish my faith and give me strength for the journey. Amen.

DO THIS IN REMEMBRANCE OF ME

The Lord's Supper is an act of receiving and remembering Christ's real presence. The night Jesus gave His disciples the bread and the wine, He told His disciples, "Do this in remembrance of Me" (Luke 22:19). Jesus instituted this Holy Meal at a feast intended for recalling God's mighty hand rescuing the Israelites from Egyptian slavery. Here are a few ways that remembering the Old Testament feast of Passover gives deeper meaning to the New Testament Sacrament:

- ✹ In the Passover feast, the Israelites were to eat unleavened bread—bread without yeast. When Pharaoh finally allowed Moses and the people of Israel to leave Egypt, they had to leave quickly. There was no time to wait for bread to rise.

- ✹ Unleavened bread symbolized purity and newness. In ancient times, the leavening process usually meant adding a bit of soured dough from a previous batch. But unleavened bread was completely new.[25] Using unleavened bread symbolized the start of a new covenant.

- ✹ Traditionally, there were four cups of wine used at the Passover meal to remember the four promises God made to the people of Israel in Exodus 6:6–7. The meal began with a blessing and the cup of sanctification. The second cup—the cup of deliverance—followed.[26]

- ✹ The third cup—the cup of redemption—came after the meal. We know this was the cup Jesus used on the night before He died, because Scripture tells us, "He took the cup, after supper, saying, 'This cup is the new covenant in My blood'" (1 Corinthians 11:25). How fitting—Jesus used the cup of redemption to institute a new covenant with His followers. His blood redeems us.

- ✹ The fourth cup of the Passover was the cup of restoration, based on God's promise, "I will take you to be My people" (Exodus 6:7). Jesus told His disciples He would not drink the fourth cup until they were all restored to Him in His kingdom (Matthew 26:29).

Soul Study

1. One of my most memorable experiences at the Lord's Table was as a youth group member actually breaking the bread and realizing the enormity of Christ's sacrifice. Talk about one of your memorable experiences of receiving Holy Communion.

2. Read Luke 22:14–23.

   a. Imagine yourself as one of the disciples reclining at the table. Describe some of the feelings and thoughts you might have experienced as you heard Jesus speak these words.

   b. Why do you think Jesus decided to institute Holy Communion on that particular night?

c. When Jesus shared the cup, He said, "Do this in remembrance of Me" (Luke 22:19). When we eat the bread and drink the cup, we remember Christ's sacrifice. What are some specific things you can do to prepare for the Lord's Supper?

3. Lord, what truth do You want me to see today?

4. Write out this week's memory verse.

Day Four

SABBATH

Remember the Sabbath day, to keep it holy.
Exodus 20:8

The year my children were five and two was one of the most tiring of my life. Of course, that is not surprising. Parenting preschoolers is an unpredictable stew of activity that has at least one predictable flavor—fatigue. But that year, I kept adding to the recipe. First, I decided to expand my piano teaching business. In addition to teaching fifteen private piano students in my home, I also began teaching a preschool music class for the local park district.

Then another musical opportunity presented itself. I was invited to be a part of a community choir and orchestra. Add in weekly rehearsals during the Christmas and Easter seasons.

In addition to all that, we added one more huge ingredient—a new home. This was the year my husband and I built a house. We were general contractors, insulators, roofers, floor installers, carpenters, and painters. Even though we hired many professionals to complete this enormous project, almost every spare minute during that year was spent hammering, sanding, varnishing, or painting.

It was no wonder that at the end of that season of life when the music classes were done, the community concerts were over, and the house was completed, that I confessed my weariness to one of my friends. I told her I felt like a squeezed-out tube of toothpaste. I had nothing left to give.

Many of us approach life with the same recipe. Take your normal work week. Add in some extra effort to propel your career. Mix in some home improvement projects. Stir in cultural or sporting events for yourself or your children. Don't forget volunteering to help your community. Final product? Exhaustion.

All the while we ignore God's instructions for life. His recipe for abundant living is simple: Take six days of work. Add in one day of rest.

God planned for us to depend on Him for daily bread. He designed His creation to find rest and sufficiency in His work and blessing. He intended that we be engaged with His Word, which sanctifies all we do. But He knew our propensity to over-schedule, and so He created the Sabbath. One day a week to rest our weary bodies. One day a week to replenish our empty souls. One day a week to soak up His love. It's a precious gift.

Yet we often turn down that gift. We think, *How can I possibly get everything done if I don't do some of it on Sunday?* The to-do list is never-ending. So Sunday becomes a catch-up day before the work week begins. One more trip to the grocery store. One (or five) more loads of laundry. One more hour on the computer to catch up on email.

I fought the idea of Sabbath for a long time. Because we are a pastor's family, Sunday is a work day for us. My husband preaches. I play the organ and piano, and I direct the choir. And since I was already working, I didn't stop when church services were over.

But one year, God worked overtime to get my attention. The idea of Sabbath kept popping up everywhere. Articles about Sabbath-keeping appeared in the magazines I read. Christian speakers talked about the benefits of Sabbath rest. I met someone at a writer's conference who was writing a book about keeping Sunday sacred.

The Father was continually tapping me on the shoulder, and finally I heard the invitation to rest. He enabled me to see my body's need for respite, my heart's need for refreshment. Now after church on Sunday, my recipe for Sabbath does not include laundry, chores, or email. Instead I stir peace into my life by resting, recharging, and refreshing.

Resting my body. For me, this means resting from work at home after Sunday services. I don't catch up on bookkeeping for piano lessons. I don't brainstorm the next chapter in my new book. I ignore the gathering dust on the coffee table. Sunday means time to do things that are not possible the rest of the week. Time to lounge on the couch and watch a movie with my hubby. Time to take a walk around the neighborhood or a leisurely hike in a state park.

Recharging my soul. One of my most renewing Sabbath practices is taking a break from technology. Not opening my overcrowded email in-box and ignoring the barrage of information on the Internet for one day a week recharges my soul.

Instead, I spend time with loved ones and catch up with distant family members by phone. I lose myself in a good book. (Okay, sometimes I use technology to read on my ereader.) Depending on my mood, I might create a special meal or heat up a frozen pizza.

Refreshing my spirit. On Sunday, I worship with my brothers and sisters in Christ. The music and the message of God's Word breathe life into my weary heart.

In fact, the best way we as Christians can keep the Sabbath holy is to sanctify it with God's Holy Word. Whatever we are doing is consecrated when we hear, read, or contemplate God's words to us. Of course, we want to allow Scripture to renovate our hearts every day of the week, but on the Sabbath, we may have more time to soak in God's life-giving Word. We can then carry God's message of love and grace into our week.

Your Sabbath might not look exactly like mine. You might need to choose a different day of the week. You might find other activities more renewing. The point is to keep the Sabbath holy. Use one day a week to reconnect with your Creator. Spend time in His Holy Word, and allow it to refresh and renew your spirit. Accept your role as the created, and receive God's gift of needed rest.

In this modern world, Sabbath-keeping is an act of courage and trust. When everyone else is working 24/7, we worry we will not be able to keep up if we work only 24/6. How will we climb the corporate ladder if we ignore our emails on Sunday? How will our children be successful if they don't participate in every Sunday sports tournament? To observe the Sabbath is to recognize our own efforts will never be enough. To remember the Sabbath is to trust God will provide.

Remember God's recipe for abundant living: Take six days of work. Add in one day of rest.

Creator God, thank You for the gift of the Sabbath. Forgive me when I have not kept this day holy, when I have not spent time in Your Word. Help me to embrace this gift of rest. Replenish my soul and renew my spirit. In Jesus' name. Amen.

Soul Study

1. Describe a typical Sunday in your house.

2. What is your reaction to God's invitation to rest one day a week?

3. What do you learn about the Sabbath in these Scriptures?
   a. Genesis 2:1–3

   b. Exodus 20:8–11

c. Isaiah 56:1–8

d. Mark 2:27–28

4. Lord, what truth do You want me to see today?

5. Write out this week's memory verse.

Day Five

CELEBRATION

*I will celebrate before the L*ORD.
2 Samuel 6:21

This summer was a whirlwind of celebration!

The fun began when my husband and I met our daughter and her family at the O'Hare airport in June. Our daughter and her husband work in China. It had been over a year since we had seen them and their three little boys. Our hearts were bursting when we were finally able to hold them in our arms.

We celebrated precious time with our grandsons by playing in the park and eating McDonald's burgers (a huge treat for the China residents). We read stories, laughed together at Winnie the Pooh videos, and squirted one another with garden hoses.

During the next month, we celebrated several birthdays with cake, balloons, and beanbag games. Little boys' faces covered in chocolate frosting. Who could ask for more than that?

In August, John and I celebrated our wedding anniversary by attending the marriage ceremony of our son! Joy spilled over at seeing Nathaniel's happiness when Mary walked down the aisle. After the beautiful ceremony, we laughed and talked and danced with family members who traveled to share the important day with us. It was a wonderful time of celebration.

Our God is a God of celebration.

For much of my life, that thought seemed incongruous with the Lord I knew. Growing up, God seemed to be a God of serious thought and solemn ceremonies, not a God of rejoicing and celebrating.

But looking closer in the Scriptures, I see God truly is a God of celebration. In the Old Testament, Yahweh commanded His chosen people to observe seven feasts each year. For three of these feasts, they were to set aside their work and travel to Jerusalem to celebrate their God (Deuteronomy 16:16). These were times of feasting and rejoicing—occasions to thank God for what He had done for them in the past and revel in the blessings He had bestowed on them in the present.

In the New Testament, Jesus was known as a partier. The Pharisees criticized Him for sharing meals with sinners (Matthew 9:11). People wondered why the Pharisees and John the Baptist's followers fasted, but Jesus' disciples went on eating and drinking (Luke 7:33–34). Parties were a favorite theme in Jesus' parables. The people in His stories celebrated finding a lost lamb, a lost coin, and a lost son (Luke 15). Jesus even compared the kingdom of God to a sumptuous banquet (Luke 14:15–24).

Too often, my worship of my generous God is sedate, somber, and dull. When God told the children of Israel to celebrate the Feast of Booths (Leviticus 23:39[27]), the Hebrew word used is *chagag*, which means "to feast, to dance, to be giddy."[28] To *chagag* is not to sit on your hands with a serious face. To *chagag* is to joyfully praise the almighty God and enthusiastically enjoy His good gifts to us.

So how can we celebrate?

We can celebrate God. Instead of absentmindedly mumbling our way through worship on Sunday, we can passionately express our love to our King. Clap along with the praise songs. Sing the hymns at the top of your lungs. To throw off restraints in celebration is a risky thing and may even feel undignified. King David was criticized by his wife, Michal, when he worshiped without inhibitions. But David was focused on praising God and not on how he looked. He told Michal, "I *will* celebrate before the LORD" (2 Samuel 6:21, emphasis mine).

We can celebrate God by observing the Church Year. Find meaningful traditions to mark the seasons. Light an Advent wreath every evening in the weeks leading up to Christmas. Make paper crowns with your kids on Epiphany. Bake unleavened bread on Maundy Thursday. Invite the neighbors over for an enormous Easter brunch, and use the opportunity to share why this is a special day.

We can celebrate God's good gifts to us. Throw a party on your birthday to celebrate God's gift of another year of life. Take your husband out for dinner to rejoice in a good work review or the completion of a big project. Lie in the grass and stare at the stars to enjoy the first night of summer. Take the kids out for ice cream to celebrate Thursday.

Enjoy the little things in life. Make a list of things that bring you joy, and include them in your ordinary days. Thank God for polka-dot teapots, lunch with friends, and time to browse in bookstores.

We can celebrate even in sorrow. Certainly, God does not expect us to dance and sing when our hearts are heavy, but we can cling to the joy we find in God even in hardship. We can memorize psalms that give God glory for who He is and recite them when we cannot find words of praise of our own. We can remember that sorrow is not the end of the story. Those who believe in Christ will celebrate at His opulent banquet for eternity.

It may seem strange to include celebration as a Spiritual *discipline*. But in celebrating what God has done for us, we lift up His name. We show the world there is joy in being a child of God, and we gladden the Father's heart. Author Donna Pyle writes, "Just as an earthly parent delights to see his or her child joyful, the most wonderful blessing we can offer God is to let His love and grace make our hearts glad."[29]

Our chaotic lives may sometimes send us to a spa as we look for rest, as we search for the strength to go on. At a spa, we can focus on things of beauty; we can concentrate on things that bring us happiness. Time away from our troubles can give us strength to come back and face them.

Remembering to celebrate a good God can also give us strength in tough times. Rejoicing in God's gracious gifts can give us strength for ordinary days. So celebrate weddings, promotions, and Thursdays. Glory in a merciful, loving, and amazing God. Joy is the fuel of our spirits.

Astonishing, remarkable, mind-blowing God—I praise You! I am sorry for the times I have been too preoccupied with my own self-importance to worship You with abandon. Forgive me for when I have neglected to celebrate the life You have given me. Help me to recklessly worship You with joy! In Jesus' name. Amen.

Soul Study

1. Talk about some of your favorite ways to celebrate with your family.

2. Write your reaction to this statement: our God is a God of celebration.

3. Read Luke 15:11–32.

    a. Why does the father celebrate (vv. 24, 32)?

    b. What is involved in the celebration (vv. 22–25)?

c. How would you describe this party?

d. Since the father in the story represents God, what does this tell you about God?

e. When have you felt like the older brother and not wanted to celebrate?

f. How could you use elements of this story in your own celebrations?

4. What are some simple ways you could incorporate more celebration into your life?

5. Lord, what truth do You want me to see today?

6. Write out this week's memory verse.

Group Activities

1. This week, we learned more and more people are rejecting traditional religion and are turning to spas as temples of wellness. Discuss the difference between secular spirituality and Christian spirituality.

2. Come back together, and discuss the week's readings and Soul Studies. Allow each woman to choose one question that speaks to her heart. She can give her answer and then open up that question to the other members of the group. Ask some of the women to share their personal worship experience from page 102.

3. Experience a short worship service together. Consider using some of these elements:

 ✿ Begin with a time of silence for everyone to center their thoughts on God.

 ✿ Dim the lights and, if possible, light some candles.

 ✿ Choose worship music that speaks to your group. Or conversely, try music out of your routine.

 ✿ Try a different worship posture. Play a loud, enthusiastic praise song or hymn, and sing at the top of your lungs with hands raised. Or play a quiet, contemplative song and kneel at your chairs with heads bowed.

 ✿ Read a psalm of praise.

 ✿ Have a time of open prayer, each woman sharing her own words of praise, glorifying God for who He is.

 ✿ If your pastor is available, include the Lord's Supper in your worship.

4. Close in prayer.

LOOSEN: LET GO OF THE IMPOSTOR

Massage

Do you need a massage? Don't you love it when someone gives you a neck rub and gets rid of all the kinks? when healing hands release the knots in your back?

At a spa, you have many massage options. Choose a Swedish relaxation massage or some deep tissue therapy. Experience thermal aroma massage or bamboo bodywork. Massage therapists might even use hot stones or their bare feet to assist in the treatment.

The whole goal of massage is to loosen tight muscles so they can move freely. Our souls may also need a loosening treatment. Often, we hold on tightly to an image that makes us feel important. We grip onto disguises because we aren't sure anyone could love who we really are.

At the Soul Spa, we want to loosen our grip on our false self and live as redeemed daughters of the King. Living free of our impostor means practicing confession—letting go of sin, which blocks our relationship with God. Abandoning our masks of self-assurance and self-importance helps uncover the true self that is loved by the Father. In discernment, we discover how to make wise, authentic choices in our complicated world. And learning the discipline of secrecy helps us loosen our people-pleasing façade.

> I would know you God, I would know myself.[30]
>
> Augustine

MEMORY VERSE

> Therefore, since we are surrounded by so great a cloud of witnesses, let us also lay aside every weight, and sin which clings so closely, and let us run with endurance the race that is set before us. Hebrews 12:1

Day One

THE IMPOSTOR VS. THE REAL YOU

*Truly, I say to you, unless you turn and become like children,
you will never enter the kingdom of heaven. Matthew 18:3*

Some of the other disciples were arguing.

Although I certainly wanted to share my opinion, I was trying to stay out of the conversation. After all, Jesus could probably hear the discussion. He was only a few steps ahead of us as we walked through the streets of Capernaum. Was He listening to the insistent murmurings behind Him?

He said nothing until we reached the house. Then, as we walked through the door, the Teacher turned around to face us, "What were you arguing about on the road?" I wanted to crawl into a hole. James and John looked at each other sheepishly. Peter stared at his feet. None of us could look Him in the eye. No one had anything to say.

Jesus sat down—a sign the Rabbi was about to teach. Now, I was sure He had known all along what the argument was about. No one had to tell Him about our petty discussion about who was the greatest.

He looked at us and said, "If anyone wants to be first in My kingdom, he must be the very last of all. He must serve everyone else."

Just then, a toddler playing in the corner of the room caught His eye. Jesus called the little boy over and had him stand in the middle of our group. Wrapping His arms around the child, He said, "Listen, unless you become like little children, you will never enter the kingdom of heaven. My kingdom is not like this world. The person who is greatest in the kingdom of heaven is the one who humbles himself like a little child. To be the greatest you must be willing to be the least."

This week, we will practice habits that help us let go of our impostor. At times, we all wear a false self that desires recognition. We put on a mask to appear important—at the cost of losing who we really are. We don a disguise because we doubt anyone could love who we are inside.

Jesus asks us to become like little children because little children don't know how to be anyone but themselves. A child is a model of lowliness, openness, and trust. Perhaps each of us was her most true self in childhood.

Let's learn about letting go of our false selves by comparing children to our impostors.

A child doesn't know how to be anyone but herself. Little kids aren't very good at deception. Mom can spot a lie a mile away. Children have not yet learned the skill of wearing a false self.

But my impostor doesn't know anything *but* the false self. My impostor tries on different identities to please other people. Living in her favorite disguises, my impostor rarely allows the real me to emerge.

A child has no status. In Jesus' time, children were viewed more as possessions than as individuals. They were insignificant and unimportant. A child in a room of adults would never have entered into a discussion about who was the greatest.

My impostor wears a false identity to appear more important. Any mask that brings greater recognition is worn often. Any disguise that garners applause is put on regularly.

A child is vulnerable and weak. A toddler often falls. Before mastering a new skill, failure is a frequent experience. But failure is not catastrophic. The two-year-old simply picks herself up off the floor and tries again.

My impostor is afraid to admit failure, terrified to confess sin. She is scared to acknowledge any kind of mistake because she is sure weakness will make her less likeable.

I often protect my impostor because I'm afraid no one will love me for who I really am—especially God.

But look at how Jesus treated the child. He took that little boy in His arms. He cared for that insignificant, weak, and probably messy child. He loved him for who he was and not for anything he had accomplished.

Jesus also embraces the real you. He invites you to let go of the impostor because the person He created you to be is the one He loves. This week, we will explore practices that help us step out of our disguises.

Just as a massage at a spa loosens our muscles, allowing us freedom of movement, living as our redeemed selves releases the grip of our impostor. Through confession and absolution, we discover the freedom of living forgiven. Through practicing authenticity, we learn to live as the women God created us to be.

Until we believe that God loves us as we are, we hold Him at arm's length. True intimacy with Christ can't occur if we doubt His affection. But when we truly believe God loves who we are under all our layers of pretense, we can accept who we are in Christ and grow in our relationship to Him.

Picture yourself as that little child Jesus calls to His side. As He puts His arms around you, feel His love for you. In the embrace, be confident that His love is for who you are and not for what you accomplish. Receive His affection for your authentic self, the real you that Jesus came to save, and not for the person you try to be. Remember you are significant to Him—and not because you are important in the world.

Father, sometimes it's hard for me to fathom that You love my flawed, imperfect, and messy self. So I try to cover up my mistakes and hide my deficiencies. I try to present a prettied-up self to You and the people around me. This week, help me to uncover the person You created me to be. Help me to be confident in Your love. In Jesus' name. Amen.

Day One

Soul Study

1. Think back to when you've experienced a massage, whether it was a professional massage done by a massage therapist or a back rub performed by your hubby. List some of the benefits you experience from massage.

2. Give your reaction to the quote: "To be nobody but myself—in a world which is doing its best, night and day, to make me somebody else—means to fight the hardest battle any human can fight, and never stop fighting." - E. E. Cummings[31]

3. Read Matthew 18:1–6; Mark 9:33–37; and Luke 9:46–48.

a. The disciples were afraid to tell Jesus what they were arguing about. Why do you think they didn't want Him to know the subject of their discussion?

b. Luke 9:47 tells us Jesus knew their thoughts. How does knowing Jesus is aware of what goes on inside our heads and hearts help or hinder our quest for authenticity?

c. Jesus used the example of a little child to teach about greatness. What is your reaction to Jesus' instruction to "turn and become like children" (Matthew 18:3)? Is that command easy or difficult for you to follow? Why?

d. It is important to note that Jesus instructs us to become childlike and not childish. *Childlike* usually carries a positive connotation, while *childish* denotes negative characteristics of children. Look up the two words and write their definitions below. Then, write in some characteristics or behaviors of each word. Finally, write how being childlike or childish would affect your relationship with God.

Word	Definition	Characteristic or behavior	How this characteristic could affect my relationship with God
childlike			
childish			

4. Lord, what truth do You want me to see today?

5. Write out this week's memory verse.

Spa Session

This week, we are exploring confession, authenticity, discernment, and secrecy. Make time in your week for one of these activities.

☼ Make an appointment for a real massage. Before you go, set aside a few minutes to read Hebrews 12:1–2. Praying through the Ten Commandments, ask God to reveal to you anything in your life that is hindering your walk with Him. Then, while receiving your massage, let go of that burden or obstruction even as your body lets go of muscle tension. Confidently receive Christ's forgiveness.

☼ Read Psalm 51—David's prayer of confession. Reread verse 6 and ask God to shine truth in your inward being. Invite Him to expose any sins you have not confessed. Ask Him to reveal the disguises you've been wearing to impress others. Write a prayer of confession.

☼ Read about the practice of secrecy (Day Five), and brainstorm some ways you could give or serve secretly. Be a "secret service" agent and do one of those acts this week.

☼ To help you discover your authentic self, make a catalog of your deepest desires. Cut out pictures from magazines that picture or symbolize your innermost longings. Examples: a picture of two women laughing depicting friendship or a photo of a sunset to show peace. After you have finished, give all these desires to God in prayer. Read Psalm 103:2–5 and remind yourself God "satisfies you with good" (v. 5). He knows your heart and will give you what is best at the right time.

Day Two

CONFESSION

*I acknowledged my sin to You, and I did not cover
my iniquity; I said, "I will confess my transgressions
to the LORD," and You forgave the iniquity of my sin.*
Psalm 32:5

I felt fantastic.

All the knots in my neck had been untied. All the tightness in my shoulders had been erased. My muscles felt as free as a kite in a spring wind.

I was so relaxed I could have fallen asleep right there on the massage table. It was as if all my anxieties had vanished along with my aches and pains. As the massage therapist removed the tension from my muscles, all the pressing responsibilities and nagging obligations in my head had also been temporarily deleted.

While talking with my therapist, I learned the breathing exercises she instructed me to do during the massage sent healing throughout my tissues. I also discovered that massage stretches weak, tight, or atrophied muscles. It increases joint flexibility and lessens stiffness. Anxiety is reduced and sleep quality is improved. Massage even releases endorphins—amino acids that work as the body's natural painkiller.

So many physical and emotional benefits are available by opening yourself to the healing touch of an expert.

At first, I was uncomfortable with the idea. I wanted the massage therapist to work out the kinks in my muscles, but I didn't like the idea of getting undressed. Although I was under a sheet, that much exposure was uncomfortable.

Confession can be the same kind of experience. It's terribly uncomfortable to expose our true self, the one who hides behind the unblemished image we work hard to protect. In our heart of hearts, we know that opening up to God will loosen the hold of our pet sins. But we would rather ignore our tendencies toward greed or envy, anger or deceit than bring them to God. Instead of letting Christ work His grace into our lives and cover over our sins with His robe of righteousness, we tightly hold onto a robe of our own making, unwilling to allow God's healing touch.

Psalm 32 is a poem of King David's attempt to cover up his sin from the holy Healer of souls.

> Blessed is the one whose transgression is forgiven,
>   whose sin is covered.
> Blessed is the man against whom the LORD counts no iniquity,
>   and in whose spirit there is no deceit.
> For when I kept silent, my bones wasted away
>   through my groaning all day long.
> For day and night Your hand was heavy upon me;
>   my strength was dried up as by the heat of summer.
> I acknowledged my sin to You,
>   and I did not cover my iniquity;
> I said, "I will confess my transgressions to the LORD,"
>   and You forgave the iniquity of my sin. Psalm 32:1–5

David experienced actual physical symptoms when he tried to cover up his sin. His "bones wasted away" and his "strength was dried up." He felt a heaviness in his soul.

I, too, sometimes try to cover up my mistakes, my apathy, my selfishness. I work hard at projecting an image everyone will like, especially God. But when I ignore the Holy Spirit's attempts to reveal a detrimental attitude, my soul begins to ache. When I pay no attention to His efforts to point out an underlying doubt, my heart wilts.

Sometimes I realize something is wrong, but I don't recognize the problem as sin. I tell myself it's simply a character flaw I need to work on. Get a self-help book and a three-point plan, and I should be able to fix this problem.

But when I'm struggling in my own strength, I am ignoring the real difficulty. I'm still carrying the burden of my sin. I am continuing the struggle to maintain a false persona—the person I want to be.

King David finally got rid of the cover-up. He said, "I will confess my transgressions to the LORD" (v. 5). When he finally let go of the pretense, he experienced the joy of grace. The words of the psalm shout out the elation of one who is forgiven, "Blessed is the one whose transgression is forgiven, whose sin is covered" (v. 1). The Hebrew word for blessed is *esher*, which can mean "happiness" or "blessedness." There is joy in realizing God no longer sees my sin. There is a lightness in my soul when I abandon the mask that tries to hide my failings.

David also said, "Blessed is the man . . . in whose spirit there is no deceit" (v. 2). At times, we are not even aware of our deceit. We may not notice hurtful attitudes. We don't admit our nagging doubts. We've worn the "good girl" robe for so long that we don't see what's underneath.

When I let go of my discomfort of exposing my body to the massage therapist, I allowed her to use her skill to soothe my aching muscles. Confession is not usually comfortable, but it reaps the benefits of wholeness, spiritual health, and a restored relationship with God.

David's experience of blessing after opening himself up to God gives us the courage to do the same. True confession means we open our hearts to God, holding His hand as we both take an honest look inside. Ask God to search your heart.

As God exposes the true condition of our souls, we allow His healing hands to begin to work. As we confess how we have failed in loving God and loving others, Christ restores our souls. He begins His work, finding the kinks and the aches. He rehabilitates our souls with His grace.

Rejoice in God's promise to forgive. Feel the happiness and blessedness of one whose sin is covered.

Holy Healer of souls, sometimes I carefully guard the image I want others to see. I'm afraid of admitting my fears, my doubts, and my failings. Help me to realize confession opens my soul to Your healing touch. Thank You for Your promise of forgiveness and grace. Amen.

Soul Study

1. Is private confession of your sins to the Father easy or difficult for you? Mark your position on the line below with an X. Why did you put your X there?

I hide behind the
unblemished image I
work hard to protect.

I'm willing to expose my sins
to the Father, for I know He
can heal me with His touch.

2. This week, when you attend worship, pay special attention to the Confession and Absolution part of the service. Arrive a few minutes early, and as you sit in the pew, ask God to reveal any sins of the past week. During Confession, silently name these sins. Rejoice in the freedom of forgiveness when the pastor speaks the words, "Jesus Christ was given to die for us, and in His stead and by His command, I forgive you all your sins." Describe your reaction to this experience here.

3. Read Psalm 32.

    a. Verse 2 says, "Blessed is the man . . . in whose spirit there is no deceit." Ask God to search your heart for any deceit. Write a prayer asking Him to reveal anything that is blocking your relationship with Him.

b. David says, "I will confess my transgressions to the Lᴏʀᴅ" (v. 5). Repent of any sins God brings to mind. Consider praying through the Ten Commandments (Exodus 20), asking God to reveal any habitual sins or underlying attitudes. Write down any sins God exposes.

c. Rejoice in God's promise to forgive, "I said, 'I will confess my transgressions to the Lᴏʀᴅ,' and You forgave the iniquity of my sin" (v. 5). Write a prayer expressing the happiness and blessedness of one forgiven.

4. Lord, what truth do You want me to see today?

5. Write out this week's memory verse.

Day Three

AUTHENTICITY

O Lord, You have searched me and known me!
Psalm 139:1

I had to have that skirt. A full-circle style in a print of mauve, green, and purple—it was the latest fashion. Searching through all the resale shops had paid off—I had an eye-catching garment at a bargain price. I was sure I would wear the skirt often. But somehow, the bold print just wasn't me. It was sprinkled with a few sequins, which made me feel self-conscious. For a person who usually dresses in classic grays and basic browns, this skirt was simply too dramatic. So the poor garment rarely sees the light of day.

I know you never make fashion mistakes like that. But I often wish the Fashion Fairy would refund my money on clothes I've never worn. Knowing your personal style is essential in avoiding the purchase of clothes you won't wear.

Even more important than identifying your personal style is knowing your authentic self. Each of us has been given a beautifully created, carefully crafted identity. A true and unique self. But most of us are convinced this identity is not good enough, and so we try on a lot of other identities—disguises that seem to get more approval or attention.

Yet we are never really comfortable in those masks. Just as I was uneasy with people looking at me in a skirt with sequins (gasp!), we are always a little uncomfortable with the attention the false self receives. *What if someone discovers I'm just faking it?*

Psalm 139 is a beautiful example of David's quest to know himself and his Creator. The shepherd-king begins with the realization God already knows him. "O Lord, You have searched me and known me!" (v. 1). Sit with that thought for a moment. God has searched your heart. He knows you inside and out. He knows what makes your soul soar. He knows what causes your heart to clench with fear. He knows what gives you unbridled hope and what sends you into cellars of despair. God already knows the authentic you.

God knows your authentic self, the sinner He sought. He loves the real you, the child who wears a brand-new identity in Christ. He is always with you, holding your hand. David says, "If I take the wings of the morning . . . Your right hand shall hold me" (vv. 9–10).

When I realize God knows my true self, I can throw off my false identities. I can toss out all the well-worn disguises when I begin to comprehend that God loves the real me—even with its weaknesses, failures, and insecurities.

Comprehending God's immense love enables us to accept ourselves as we are. Psalm 139 goes on, "I praise You, for I am fearfully and wonderfully made" (v. 14). When we experience God's acceptance, we are able to appreciate the true self as a gift of God's creative genius. The true self is not something we can manufacture out of accomplishments or build with an amazing résumé. If I can see myself as "fearfully and wonderfully made," I am less likely to cover up God's handiwork with my own disguises.

Knowing the true self doesn't mean we become self-absorbed, however. In the middle of the psalm, David expresses his desire to know God. "How precious to me are Your thoughts, O God! How vast is the sum of them!" (v. 17). We can only know ourselves better by knowing God better. As our relationship with God deepens, we begin to know His character. And the more we know the Lord, the more we are able to trust Him. The more we comprehend God's goodness, the more we are able to drop our pretense and come to Him simply as ourselves.

David ends the psalm with a plea, "Search me, O God, and know my heart! Try me and know my thoughts! And see if there be any grievous way in me, and lead me in the way everlasting!" (vv. 23–24). Since David stated at the beginning of the psalm that God had already searched his heart, I think this prayer is a request for God to let David in on the search. Confidence that God loves the real me gives me the boldness to ask God to search my heart. Faith that He will never abandon me provides the bravery to ask Him to show me where my anxieties are preventing me from being the person HE created me to be. Appreciation for His creative work enables me to ask Him to point out where I have left the path He intended me to take so I can get back on "the way everlasting."

Yes, this may seem a little scary. God may point out pet sins we don't want to give up. He asks us to abandon identities that have become a part of us. But once we have let them go, we will experience the freedom of being our true selves.

Although we're tempted to clothe our authentic self with false identities, we need to remember that God knows the old self that He sent Christ to redeem and save. The Father loves the beautiful, delightful, amazing, wonderful *real* you, the flawed, insecure, and weak you. In fact, coming to God in our weaknesses is the way to experience God's love and acceptance. Martin Luther writes:

> For by this commandment God lets us plainly understand that He will not cast us away from Him or chase us away [Romans 11:1]. This is true even though we are sinners. But instead He draws us to Himself [John 6:44], so that we might humble ourselves before Him [1 Peter 5:6], bewail this misery and plight of ours, and pray for grace and help [Psalm 69:13].[32]

When I'm brave enough to come to God without any bold prints to cover up my self-doubt, I know I am loved for who I am. When I'm courageous enough to approach Him without any sequins to attract attention, I can experience being accepted exactly as God created me to be.

Father in heaven, "I praise You, for I am fearfully and wonderfully made." Sometimes I don't recognize this truth, but I thank You for creating me just as I am. Search my heart, and expose any false identities preventing me from truly knowing Your love and acceptance. In Jesus' name. Amen.

Soul Study

1. Do you own a piece of clothing you hardly ever wear because it doesn't express your personality? Describe it.

2. What persona do you sometimes wear to get more attention or approval?

3. Read Psalm 139, prayerfully asking God to search your heart and let you in on the process. Answer these questions to help uncover the real you.
   a. How do you want people to see you?

   b. Verse 1 says, "O LORD, You have searched me and known me!" God perceives the real you. How do you think He sees you in His eyes of grace?

c. Read verses 9–10. If you were confident God was holding your hand, what disguises might you be willing to let go?

d. Verse 14 says, "I praise You, for I am fearfully and wonderfully made." Most of us have difficulty believing this. Which of your personality traits or character qualities are hard for you to accept?

e. Write a prayer bringing all your disguises, insecurities, and worries to God. Thank Him that He loves you just as you are.

4. Lord, what truth do You want me to see today?

5. Write out this week's memory verse.

Day Four

DISCERNMENT

And it is my prayer: that your love may abound more and more, with knowledge and all discernment, so that you may approve what is excellent, and so be pure and blameless for the day of Christ.
Philippians 1:9–10

Discern what is best. With the myriad of choices in our modern world, this is a difficult task. We have hundreds of options for spending our money and our time. How do we choose what is best?

We want to give our children the finest of experiences and education. Should we sign them up for ballet or basketball, soccer or sewing class, painting or piano? While this music teacher puts in a vote for piano lessons (smile), we realize these are all fine choices. And so we pack the schedule with as many good things as we can.

There are many options for personal development as well. We could sign up for book clubs, Bible studies, and knitting groups. Exercise classes, civic organizations, cooking classes all sound inviting.

We see a world in need. Children in third-world countries, sex-trafficking victims, and homeless people in our community all require help. We want to make a difference in the world so we sign up for cancer walks and serving at soup kitchens. We hear Christ's call to serve and go on short-term mission trips and volunteer to work with the church youth group.

It doesn't take long before we are overwhelmed.

Last year, I said yes to too many things. In addition to my writing and speaking career, I continued to teach a dozen piano students, play piano for church services, and direct our congregation's choir. I participated in a local Toastmasters group and a music teachers' organization. I led a weekly Bible study at my church and joined another group of women that met twice a month to study Scripture and discuss how we could make a difference to people in extreme poverty. I started volunteering at a local homeless shelter for women.

And it all became too much.

I'm sure you could also tell me a tale of an overstuffed life. Have you noticed when you ask someone the simple question "How are you?" that one of the most common answers is "Busy!"?

A life too full of doing has little time for being. How can we learn to make wise choices? How can we discern what is best? How can we live in sync with the life God wants for us?

First of all, we discern what is best by praying "Thy will be done." I put discernment in the category of "Loosen" because we can discern God's will only when we're ready to let go of our own. When we are prepared to release our own personal agendas and priorities, we will be more open to God's leading.

We can pray that most daring of prayers—Thy will be done—only when we are moved by love. In the passage above, the apostle Paul prays for the Philippians' love to abound because he knows following God's will wholeheartedly happens when we are motivated by love—love for God and love for His people. At times, we can make ourselves do what is right, but we may not be able to persevere in the action if our heart isn't in it. So Paul prays for love—love that abounds in knowledge. The better we know God and His love, the more our love will increase. And the more our love increases, the more we will *want* what God wants.

When my calendar overflowed, I needed to examine my motives for saying yes to so many activities. Had I prayed about each new commitment? Or had I jumped in because I wanted the pat on the back that came with that responsibility? I had to admit not all of the activities were motivated by love.

We discern what is best by reading God's Word. Scripture is "a lamp to my feet and a light to my path" (Psalm 119:105). When I'm struggling with a choice, I first look to the Bible for any commandments or clear instructions on my options. Sometimes, there is a clear right and wrong in the choices in front of me, but this time, all the possibilities before me were good ones. The Bible tells us to serve one another and to develop our gifts.

So I needed to look for scriptural principles to guide me. Clearly, I wasn't paying attention to the instruction "So teach us to number our days that we may get a heart of wisdom" (Psalm 90:12). While on earth, we live in a world of time—twenty-four hours a day for every person. I had packed my schedule as if I had thirty-six-hour days and was wondering why it wasn't working.

We discern what is best through the counsel of wise Christians. Proverbs 12:15 says, "The way of a fool is right in his own eyes, but a wise man listens to advice." When we are searching for specific guidance, it is helpful to talk things out with your pastor or a Christ-centered friend. Scripture doesn't have any passages that say "Take the job in Dayton" or "Don't marry Fred," but turning to mature Christians can help us sort out our choices.

I admitted to some friends that I was feeling overwhelmed. They confessed they were struggling with the same issue. We took time to pray for guidance and for the ability to follow God's leading.

We discern what is best through turning toward God. A fundamental task in discernment is to pay attention to the state of our hearts: Are they turned toward God? Or away from Him?

I love the promise in Isaiah 26:3, "You keep him in perfect peace whose mind is stayed on You, because he trusts in You." The Hebrew for the verb *stayed* is *camak* and means "to lean, lay, rest, support, put, uphold, lean upon."[33] How can my mind experience peace in my choices? By resting on God, by leaning on His support. When I am turned toward God and leaning on His strength, I experience His peace. I receive a tranquility that can come only from the God worthy of my trust.

But when I lean on something other than God—my own abilities or ambition for instance—I feel anxiety. When I turn away from God, I lose His peace. I become more self-obsessed and may even experience sadness or depression. A lack of quiet in my soul may be a sign that I am not resting on God.

To discern the best choices in my life, I began to pay more attention to my attitude as I progressed through my week. Did this activity give me joy and peace? Or was that slot in my schedule life-draining? Did I serve out of love? Or was my motivation something else entirely—guilt, obligation, or a ploy for attention? As I prayed for God's guidance and noticed which activities brought me closer to my Savior and which pulled me away, the choices became clearer.

This is not to say that everything God asks us to do will be simple. But when we're following God's way for our lives, it will be more like walking with Him, rather than pulling against His leading.

Discern what is best. In the countless options of this complicated world, take time to choose wisely. Pray "Thy will be done" and search God's Word for guidance. Seek out the wisdom of mature brothers and sisters in Christ. Pay attention to Christ's leading. Are the choices you make drawing you closer to Him or pulling you away? Follow out of love for the Savior, who loved and died for you.

Savior, forgive me when I have filled my schedule so full there is no room for You. Give me discernment for what is best. I want to choose those things that draw me closer to You. Because I trust Your love, I pray, "Thy will be done." Amen.

Day Four

Soul Study

1. Make a list of all the activities you do on a weekly or monthly basis. Include the things you do for others (e.g. driving your daughter to tennis lessons or taking your mother shopping).

2. Take a moment to contemplate each activity. Rate each activity from 1 to 5, 1 being the most soul-draining and 5 being the most life-giving.

3. Spend some time praying over your schedule for the coming week. Request wisdom in discerning what is best. Ask God to show you if any changes need to be made.

4. Psalm 25 is a practical instruction manual in learning discernment. Read verses 4–12 and use the SACRED reading process we discovered in Week 2 to listen to God's Word to you.

> **Silence your thoughts.** (Allow your mind to quiet down.)
>
> **Attend to the passage.** (Read the passage out loud, pausing when the Spirit brings a part of it to your attention.)
>
> **Contemplate the Word.** (Meditate on the passage, asking, "How does this passage speak to my life?")
>
> **Respond to the text.** (Pray, pouring out your heart to God in response to what you have read.)
>
> **Exhale and rest.** (Read the text again and simply rest in the love of God.)
>
> **Dwell in the Word.** (Take a truth or promise with you into your day.)

5. Lord, what truth do You want me to see today?

6. Write out this week's memory verse.

Day Five

SECRECY

*But when you give to the needy, do not let your left hand know
what your right hand is doing, so that your giving may be in secret.
And your Father who sees in secret will reward you.*
Matthew 6:3—4

In the writing world, we writers are expected to self-promote. We blog. We engage in social media. To let others know about our books, we do interviews and schedule book signings.

Most likely, there are times when you also need to sound the trumpet about your latest accomplishments. To get ahead in the corporation, you need to let your boss know about the extra work you put in on the latest project. You inspire others in your volunteer group by telling them how you served your community.

In our society, working in secrecy is a foreign concept. Businesses use flashing neon signs to promote their product. Politicians blather endlessly about what they've done for their constituents. Public figures hire PR people to market their best image.

The discipline of secrecy is deliberately deciding not to promote ourselves and our good deeds. In *The Spirit of the Disciplines*, Dallas Willard says, "Secrecy rightly practiced enables us to place our public relations department entirely in the hands of God."[34] When we do acts of love or generosity in Jesus' name without receiving any credit, we are practicing secrecy.

This isn't easy. It's difficult to work on the sidelines. It's challenging when you give your all and no one notices. We want the pat on the back, the recognition at the charity banquet, the mention in the local paper.

Jesus often spoke about serving without compensation or recognition. Some of His harshest words were about the hypocrites of His day who worked only for the applause of men. In fact, one entire section of His Sermon on the Mount is dedicated to this topic.

Thus, when you give to the needy, sound no trumpet before you, as the hypocrites do in the synagogues and in the streets, that they may be praised by others. Truly, I say to you, they have received their reward. But when you give to the needy, do not let your left hand know what your right hand is doing, so that your giving may be in secret. And your Father who sees in secret will reward you. Matthew 6:2–4

Jesus' words challenge me to examine my motives in giving and serving. Am I sharing out of love or out of a need for attention? Secretly serving loosens my impostor. It helps me to step out of the restricting mask of people-pleasing and wear a true gown of service.

Jesus told the crowd on the mount that when we trumpet our giving so we are praised in public, we have already received our reward. God rewards the deeds done in secret. But truthfully, I sometimes value recognition from people more than some ethereal, heavenly gold star I can't imagine.

That's when I must remember that working for the approval of people has other effects on my life. Working for the admiration of others is a never-ending quest, because just as I receive one reward, I will start looking for the next. When I see a co-worker getting a bigger trophy or more substantial raise, I will be crippled with the comparison disease. I will experience the bitter pain of disappointment if no one notices the amazing things I've done.

But I begin to learn the true joy of simple service when I stay behind the scenes. When I let go of the need for applause from others, I play to the Audience of One and rejoice in His blessing.

A massage at the spa releases the toxins our muscles hold onto. Practicing secrecy enables us to rid our lives of the poison of people-pleasing. Jesus invites us to live free of wondering what people think of us.

As we empty our souls of the need for recognition, we make more room for the Holy Spirit to work. We leave space for a greater dependence on God. As we let Jesus handle our public relations department, we experience a soul transformation.

Jesus, I confess I sometimes value the applause from people more than Your approval. Help me today to step out of the prison of people-pleasing. Show me secret acts of service I can do for the people in my life. In Your Holy name. Amen.

HOW CAN WE PRACTICE THE DISCIPLINE OF SECRECY?

☼ ***Before you decide to give or serve, examine your motives.*** Are you contributing simply for attention or approval? Or are you doing it out of love for others and obedience to God?

☼ ***When the opportunity arises, volunteer for behind-the-scenes jobs.*** Set up tables, wash dishes, or send out invitations. Ask that your name be omitted from the program.

☼ ***Do a service for someone without letting them know who did it.*** Take out the garbage can for your son. Mow the neighbors' lawn while they're away. Buy a pastry for a co-worker and put it on her desk before she gets to work.

☼ ***Institute a week of "secret service" at home.*** Encourage your family to do small secret services for one another. Make someone's bed. Leave anonymous gifts on pillows. Tuck encouraging notes in backpacks and briefcases.

☼ ***Send someone an unsigned gift.*** Get a money order or grocery store gift card, and mail it with an encouraging card. To disguise who it's from, write with your other hand or have someone else in your family address the envelope.

Day Five

Soul Study

1. Have you ever received an anonymous gift? What effect did it have on you?

2. Our human nature wants the spotlight to shine on our accomplishments. All of us struggle with approval addiction. Here are a few questions to ask yourself to determine the level of your dependence on people-pleasing. Mull over these questions, and journal any discoveries you made about yourself.

    a. Do I feel disappointed when no one notices my work?

    b. Do I get upset if someone else takes credit for my idea?

    c. Do I find myself volunteering for a task so people will think I'm gifted, generous, organized, and so on?

    d. Do I pout if no one thanks me for my work?

3. Read Matthew 6:1–18.

    a. What three things are we to do in secret (vv. 3, 5, 16)?

b. How can practicing these things openly exemplify a desire for public approval?

c. What is your reaction to verse 4? Is it easy or difficult for you to work in secret?

d. We do not always do these things secretly. There is a time for public prayer. Sometimes, we unite with other believers to fast for a specific purpose. How can doing them secretly help us during the times we do them publicly?

4. Lord, what truth do You want me to see today?

5. Write out this week's memory verse.

Group Activities

1. Do a group massage. Stand in a circle. Have everyone turn to the right side and put their hands on the shoulders of the person in front of them. Everyone rubs the shoulders of that person for two minutes. Then, turn and massage the shoulders of the person on the left.

2. Discuss the week's readings and Soul Studies. Allow each woman to choose one question that speaks to her heart. After she gives her answer, open up that question to the other members of the group. Ask some of the women to share their experience with the Spa Session activities from page 127.

3. Open up a time of confession.

   ☼ Give everyone a piece of paper.

   ☼ Begin by reading Psalm 139:23–24: "Search me, O God, and know my heart! Try me and know my thoughts! And see if there be any grievous way in me, and lead me in the way everlasting!"

   ☼ Allow time for everyone to quietly reflect on their past day or week and to write down sins God reveals.

   ☼ Consider dividing into groups of two or three and confessing to one another. Sometimes, there is healing in confessing to another Christian.

   ☼ When everyone is finished, destroy the papers in some way: burn them, put them through a shredder, or nail them to a wooden cross, remembering Christ's complete destruction of our sins.

   ☼ Close the confession time hearing God's words of forgiveness by reading Psalm 103 aloud as a group.

4. Close in prayer.

SHARE:
PARTICIPATE IN THE LIVES OF OTHERS

Manicure

A visit to the nail salon is a beautiful part of a stay at the spa. Professional nail technicians trim and shape nails. They rub away ragged cuticles and rough calluses. Nail polish or lacquer is expertly applied. You might even have the opportunity to enjoy a relaxing hand or foot massage.

We use our hands and feet to participate in the lives of others. Our hands bake loaves of banana bread for the bake sale to raise money for church ministries. Our feet run 5Ks to support battered women's shelters. Tired hands tie tiny shoes and spoon food into aged mouths. Aching feet walk the halls of hospitals. We extend the hand of fellowship in our churches and hold the hand of a grieving friend.

We were not meant to live in isolation. God has placed us in families and churches to support us and refine us. This week, we will learn about Spiritual disciplines that involve sharing: service, hospitality, fellowship, and mentoring.

> Others . . . become agents of grace in our growth toward wholeness in Christ, while we become agents of God's grace in their growth.[35]
>
> Robert Mulholland

MEMORY VERSE
> *Iron sharpens iron, and one man sharpens another.*
> Proverbs 27:17

Day One

LOVE TO THE END

If I then, your Lord and Teacher, have washed your feet,
you also ought to wash one another's feet. For I have given you
an example, that you also should do just as I have done to you.
John 13:14–15

It was time for the Passover meal. The rest of the disciples and I shuffled into an upper room we had prepared. Hot and tired from walking the streets of Jerusalem all day, I plopped down onto a cushion and leaned against the wooden table.

Wine was passed. Food was shared. We spoke the sacred words that had been repeated for millenia: "It is the sacrifice of the Lord's Passover."

Suddenly, in the middle of the meal, Jesus stood up, peeled off His outer robe, and wrapped a long towel around His waist. He poured water into the basin by the door and moved it toward Matthew. As He gently took Matthew's feet and put them in the basin, I cringed. *The Master washing feet? It shouldn't be.* Looking around the room, I saw all eyes lowered. One of us should have volunteered to wash the grime of the streets off everyone's feet as we entered. But probably each disciple was feeling as I was hot, tired, and . . . self-important. No one wanted to take on the job of the lowest servant.

Jesus continued down the line of disciples seated at the table—James, Philip, Bartholomew. I was next.

"Lord, are You going to wash my feet?" I asked.

"Peter, you can't understand what I am doing now, but later it will all make sense." He lifted my foot to put it into the water.

I pulled it away, "No! You will never wash my feet!"

Jesus looked me in the eye, "Then you can have no part of Me."

Those words stabbed me in the heart. "Then Lord, wash my head and hands along with my feet!"

When all twenty-four feet were clean, Jesus returned to His seat. Leaning in toward us and resting on His elbows, He said, "Do you see what I have done for you? You call Me Teacher and Lord—and that is what I am. But I have shown you that if I, your Lord and Teacher, can wash your feet, you should do the same for one another. Serve one another—this is how your life will be blessed."

I'm a little squeamish about feet. I could never work at a spa or salon as a nail technician. Give someone a pedicure? Touch a stranger's feet? I don't think so.

Yet Jesus bent down to wash two dozen feet. Feet caked with the dust of Jerusalem's streets. Why did He stoop, both literally and figuratively, to do this dirty and demeaning job? Jesus told His disciples—and us—His purpose in John 13:14–15:

> If I then, your Lord and Teacher, have washed your feet, you also ought to wash one another's feet. For I have given you an example, that you also should do just as I have done to you.

Jesus washed dirty feet to teach servanthood. What principles of service can we learn from His example?

In serving, we show love. John 13:1 tells us that when this Passover meal neared, Jesus knew He would soon be leaving the world. It was time to go back to the Father, but not before He showed His love to the twelve men with whom He had shared His life for the past three years. "Having loved His own who were in the world, He loved them to the end" (John 13:1b). He saved a dramatic demonstration of His love for the finish line of His life.

We can tell others "I love you," but it is service that demonstrates the full extent of our love. Being willing to rearrange your schedule to give someone a ride. Taking care of a friend who is ill. Getting down and dirty to help a neighbor clean up their basement after a flood. All of these acts of service display love.

In serving, we live out our purpose and position. John 13:3–4 says, "Jesus, knowing that the Father had given all things into His hands, and that He had come from God and was going back to God, rose from supper. He laid aside His outer garments, and taking a towel, tied it around His waist." Jesus didn't respond to the fact that all things were given to Him by ordering others around. Instead, He willingly took the role of a servant. The way

John puts it makes it seem like washing feet was the next logical step in being Lord of the universe. Mind-boggling.

This is how God wants us to respond as well. The Book of Ephesians tells us that because of Christ, God has "raised us up with Him and seated us with Him in the heavenly places in Christ Jesus" (Ephesians 2:6). We are children of the King, heirs to the eternal kingdom. But we are not to use this position in arrogance and self-satisfaction. We are to live out our purpose to serve. We are "created in Christ Jesus for good works, which God prepared beforehand" (Ephesians 2:10).

In serving, we do what is needed. Foot washing was normally performed by a servant, usually the lowest-ranked slave in the house. But at the Passover feast in the Upper Room, there was no servant. Certainly, all of the disciples were aware of this fact. One of them should have volunteered for the job, but they all walked past the pitcher and basin. Jesus did what was needed. He washed grubby feet.

A true servant will not dictate which jobs he will do and not do. He will obey his Lord. He will do what is needed.

In serving, we lay aside our pride. In taking off His outer robe, Jesus gave us a picture of shedding our pride. Humility is the garment of service.

Jesus was willing to do the lowliest job. Am I? Or do I only sign up for assignments that will be noticed? Do I only accept work that will be applauded?

In serving, we receive God's blessing. Jesus told the disciples, "If you know these things, blessed are you if you do them" (John 13:17). We may not receive a trophy or a paycheck for taking on the tasks of humble service, but we will receive God's blessing. Serving is the way of Christ. Service is what puts a smile on God's face.

Although I'm still not sure I'm up for the task of foot washing, I am asking God to give me the heart of a servant. Knowing I am a child of the King helps me to lay aside my pride and do what is necessary. I serve to please my Lord.

Jesus, I thank You for Your example of humble service. Help me to live out my purpose and position as a child of the King by serving the people around me. Help me to do what is needed even if it is the lowliest job. Give me Your grace to complete the tasks You give me. In Your name. Amen.

Soul Study

1. Have you ever had a manicure or pedicure? What is your reaction to someone serving you in this way?

2. How does remembering your position as child of the King help you to take on menial tasks?

3. Read John 13:1–17.

   a. Imagine yourself in the position of one of the disciples. Describe your reaction when Jesus came to wash your feet.

   b. Jesus washed the disciples' feet to demonstrate His love. What is one thing God has done for you lately that has displayed His love for you?

c. Washing feet was one of the lowliest jobs, yet Jesus did it to show His love. What is one of your most despised tasks? How could doing it in love change it for you?

d. Think of a small service you could do for someone today. Write it here and find time to carry it out.

4. Lord, what truth do You want me to see today?

5. Write out this week's memory verse.

Spa Session

This week, we are exploring the disciplines of service, hospitality, fellowship, and mentoring. Make room in your schedule for one of these soul-stretching activities:

✿ Read Philippians 2:1–11. Think about a service you are already doing. Write a prayer asking God to help you be a Christlike servant in that role.

✿ Read Isaiah 61:1–2. How could you or your group serve one of the groups of people mentioned in that passage? Brainstorm some ideas and decide to carry one of them out.

✿ After reading about soul guides (Day Five), send a card to someone who has been an important guide in your spiritual life. Include a picture of the two of you if possible.

✿ Initiate a time of fellowship. Invite people to your home or arrange for a night out with friends. Encourage lots of talk and laughter.

Day Two

SERVICE

Have this mind among yourselves, which is yours in Christ Jesus,
who, though He was in the form of God, did not count equality
with God a thing to be grasped, but emptied Himself, by taking
the form of a servant, being born in the likeness of men.
Philippians 2:5—7

During my stay at the spa, I had my first manicure. Some of you are probably wondering how I could have waited decades for such a necessary service. But you see, my hands play the piano—my nails must be clipped short. My hands dig in my garden—dirt and nail polish don't coexist very well. My hands wash a lot of dishes—why bother with a manicure that will only get chipped right away?

But at the spa, I decided to treat myself. So what if the manicure wouldn't last? I wanted my nails to look nice—just once.

Having never experienced this luxury before, I was fascinated by the process. I was amazed that the manicure lasted forty-five minutes! Who knew it took so long to do it right? The nail technician shaped my nails and rubbed off rough cuticles. She massaged my hands with lotion. She applied a pretty pink polish and tipped each nail with white. The French manicure actually gave the illusion of length.

As I chatted with the manicurist, I couldn't help but realize that as this kind woman was making my hands more comfortable and beautiful, she was using her own hands, probably to their detriment. She told me she rarely used polish herself because using nail polish remover all day meant her polish came off in the process. She admitted she often had aching hands at the end of the day and nothing felt as good to her as a hand massage.

When we serve, we are putting others' needs ahead of our own, just as my manicurist made my hands beautiful at the expense of her own.

We all serve others in one way or another. Maybe you're a mom, serving your family by cooking meals, washing clothes, and sweeping up the remains of breakfast from the floor. Perhaps you work in a shop serving customers all day. Or it could be that you serve in a church, tending to the needs of your brothers and sisters in Christ.

Service as a Spiritual discipline is not so much about what we do, but how and why we do it. Do I serve out of duty or out of love for God and His people? Do I serve to get my name on a program or to become more Christlike? Is my goal to grow in fame or in humility?

Philippians 2:3–7 says:

> Do nothing from selfish ambition or conceit, but in humility count others more significant than yourselves. Let each of you look not only to his own interests, but also to the interests of others. Have this mind among yourselves, which is yours in Christ Jesus, who, though He was in the form of God, did not count equality with God a thing to be grasped, but emptied Himself, by taking the form of a servant, being born in the likeness of men.

Serving as a Spiritual discipline is viewing service as an opportunity to grow in humility. I could serve at a local homeless shelter to get my name in the program at the year-end banquet. I could help out in order to get those good feelings of making a difference. Or I could serve because I see the women in the shelter as precious children of God, even though their current circumstances are not especially glamorous.

Serving as a Spiritual discipline means not simply looking at our own interests. We might have an idea of where we want to help out, but growing in faith through service means taking the time to ask God to show us where He wants us to serve. Perhaps your interest is in short-term foreign missions, but after praying, you consider God may be leading you to teach refugees in your hometown. Or you might discover that although you have a burden to help your community and world, God is calling you to concentrate your sphere of service to your babies and toddlers for now.

Serving as a Spiritual discipline requires asking God for "the attitude of Christ" and the "form of a servant." This is not natural for us as selfish humans. Taking on the nature of a servant means being aware of the needs of others. It involves asking God to show me someone to serve instead of expecting others to serve me. At work, I will make the coffee instead of waiting for someone else to do it. At home, I will empty the dishwasher before my husband does.

Serving as a Spiritual discipline is accepting service as a chance to become more Christlike. We do this whenever we serve in love as Christ did. A young mom prepares the meals, cleans the house, and changes the diapers. She could do it as a means to check off tasks on her to-do list. She could do it because "someone has to." Or she could do it as a way to demonstrate her love to her family. Even our mundane chores can become a way to become more Christlike if we do them out of thanksgiving for the people in our lives. Making others feel special is a way to demonstrate the outlandish love of God.

Just as the manicurist at the spa sacrificed her own hands to make mine beautiful, we can make small daily sacrifices to enhance the lives of others. And when we act in love, service becomes an opportunity to grow in humility and Christlikeness. It is a chance to follow God's heart for us and to learn the nature of a servant.

Dearest Savior, You left the glory of heaven to come to our dusty world. You willingly took the role of a servant. Give me a servant attitude. Help me to be aware of the needs in my world and find someone I can serve today. In Your name. Amen.

Day Two

Soul Study

1. When, in your experience, has service helped you become more Christlike?

2. The story of the Good Samaritan is a picture of service in love. Read the story in Luke 10:30–37.

a. Take time to picture yourself in the story: first as the priest or Levite, then the Samaritan, and finally as the crime victim. Think about your reactions to what is happening, your emotions, and your motives. Write down what you discover about each character below.

Priest or Levite

Samaritan

Crime victim

b. Which character do you most identify with? Why?

c. In light of this story, how does service change us? Think of service in terms of both serving and being served.

3. Lord, what truth do You want me to see today?

4. Write out this week's memory verse.

Day Three

HOSPITALITY

*Contribute to the needs of the saints and
seek to show hospitality. Romans 12:13*

How do you define *hospitality?* Does it mean crystal goblets and fine china? Or are paper plates allowed? Is a seven-course meal necessary? Or does a frozen pizza count?

One of my most authentic experiences with hospitality occurred when a missionary family came to speak at our church one Sunday. Everyone was fascinated by the stories of their lives in Africa. The family stayed long after the service describing their work and answering questions.

My husband, John, and I immediately connected with the couple. Apart from the places we lived, we had much in common. So after the rest of the congregation left and my husband began locking up the church, I realized I wanted to continue our conversation. And as the noon hour neared, I suspected this family didn't have lunch plans.

The pastor's wife side of me thought: *You should invite them over for lunch. They probably want something to eat.*

But the introverted, perfectionist side of me argued: *Remember what the house looked like when you left this morning? You don't want them to see that. No food has been prepared. You should have thought of this before.*

Surprisingly, my pastor's wife self spoke up first, "Why don't you come over for lunch?"

And so, this family entered our slightly cluttered house. They helped my husband get more chairs around the dining room table. The wife assisted my daughter in setting out plates and silverware. I whipped up a double batch of waffle batter and defrosted some pork sausages.

When a few waffles were ready to eat, we all sat down in the dining room and shared the simple meal. I kept popping into the kitchen to get more waffles as they were done.

Conversation flowed along with the maple syrup. Even my introverted self was having a wonderful time with these people we had just met. In fact, we laughed and talked so much I completely forgot about the last waffle until we started clearing the table and carrying dishes into the kitchen.

There we saw the waffle maker belching black smoke. Lifting the lid revealed a charred and blackened pastry.

John grabbed a pair of tongs. "I'll take care of that," he said as he carried the burnt mess away.

Looking back on that incident, I think it was one of the few times I have been able to offer true hospitality.

It's not that I never invite people to my home. I invite friends over for coffee and dessert. Occasionally, I host Christmas parties and spring brunches for the women of our church. My extended family has spent many holidays in our home.

But those events are sometimes more about entertaining than hospitality. I can easily get stressed about having a spotless home and a tantalizing menu. Hours may be spent cooking, baking, and arranging the table just so. I might get so focused on the getting the dinner rolls out of the oven on time that I forget to pay attention to the people in my home.

Inviting the missionary family over that Sunday afternoon was definitely not about entertaining. Toys on the floor, dishes in the sink, papers on the kitchen table—my guests were not going to be impressed by an immaculate home. No elaborate menu had been prepared—an impromptu breakfast was all we had to offer. I had no time to plan ahead—no one could be awestruck by my organizational skills.

Yet, during that little brunch, I was so focused on my delightful guests that I completely ignored the burning waffle in the kitchen.

While entertaining is done to impress, hospitality is done out of love. Entertaining dazzles; hospitality serves. Entertaining amazes; hospitality shares.

The Book of Romans tells us we, as Christians, are to practice hospitality.

> Let love be genuine. Abhor what is evil; hold fast to what is good. Love one another with brotherly affection. Outdo one another in showing honor. Do not be slothful in zeal, be fervent in spirit, serve the Lord. Rejoice in hope, be patient in tribulation, be constant in prayer. Contribute to the needs of the saints and seek to show hospitality. Romans 12:9–13

Hospitality can be a Spiritual discipline if it stretches us to love others as Christ loves them. It increases faith as we step out of our comfort zone to invite someone to our home who may not be able to return the favor. It helps us to grow closer to the Savior as we share the blessings He has given us.

Many versions of the Bible translate the last part of verse 13 as "practice hospitality." I like that. "Practicing hospitality" means we're still working on that skill; we haven't perfected it yet. We can invite people over when the house is messy. We can share a meal even if we aren't Martha Stewart.

Practicing hospitality also means doing it regularly. Look for opportunities to share food and fellowship with friends. Find ways to bless people who may not be able to bless you back.

When we practice hospitality, we may chip a nail or two. Our hands may grow tired. But we will also gain the shine that comes from sharing life with others. Our lives will exhibit a brilliance that cannot be had in isolation.

Now back to that blackened waffle. When my husband took that burnt offering out to the garage, I assumed he was throwing it into the garbage can. However, the next Sunday it reappeared in the pulpit as an illustration for my husband's sermon entitled, "Well done."

Let us all practice true hospitality that is "well done."

Father in heaven, forgive me when I have not shared what You have given me. Help me to learn hospitality is not about fancy dishes, but about showing Your love to Your Body. Teach me to share with even the least of these. In Jesus' name. Amen.

Soul Study

1. Talk about a time you experienced true hospitality, whether giving it or receiving it.

2. What are some specific ways you could practice hospitality? How could you welcome others into your heart and home to extend the love of Christ? Brainstorm some ideas with your group.

3. Read Romans 12:9–16.
   a. Write down all the phrases from this passage that could apply to hospitality.

   b. Which of those elements mean the most to you when you are in someone's home?

c. Verse 9 says love must be sincere. Describe hospitality that shows sincere love, and then contrast that with hospitality that is insincere.

d. The Greek word translated hospitality is *philoxenia,* which literally means "love to strangers." Although it is not always wise to invite strangers to our homes, brainstorm some ways you could practice *philoxenia.*

4. Lord, what truth do You want me to see today?

5. Write out this week's memory verse.

Day Four

FELLOWSHIP

Iron sharpens iron, and one man sharpens another.
Proverbs 27:17

Consider these two scenarios.

A small group of women gathers together every Wednesday night to study the Bible. Tea, banana bread, and laughter are often shared along with grace, encouragement, and true confessions. Each woman leaves blessed by the others.

One congregational member would look forward to going to church to experience fellowship with the Body of Christ except for the fact that she is almost certain to encounter one particularly difficult part of the Body. That part of the body is often rude and hurtful. Extra grace is always required, and the effort is draining.

What do these two situations have in common? First of all, they are both circumstances I have experienced. And it's a pretty safe bet that you have faced both of these situations as well. Christian fellowship can be invigorating and healing or it can be disappointing and challenging.

Second, both scenarios describe why Christian fellowship is necessary to our spiritual growth. We need one another to prop us up in the hard times and to encourage us as we walk together in faith. But being a part of the Body of Christ is not always easy, and it is in those times God uses other people to refine us and to teach us to lean on Him.

Proverbs 27:17 says, "Iron sharpens iron, and one man sharpens another." God designed us to need one another. He uses the Body of Christ to refine and hone our faith and trust. In her book *The Busy Mom's Guide to Spiritual Survival*, Kelli Trujillo writes:

> When we live isolated lives, absent of real fellowship,
> we relinquish the very tool God would use to prod us
> along in growing as disciples of Jesus.[36]

Fellowship is a Spiritual discipline because it helps us connect to Christ through His Body of believers. Being part of a community of disciples supports our efforts to live out all the other Spiritual disciplines.

Think of fellowship as the nail file in a manicure. Community sharpens our faith. Fellowship rubs off our rough edges.

Fellowship rubs off our sadness and isolation. As we gather with other Christians in Bible study, we are encouraged in our faith. When we unite in worship, our joy and zeal are rekindled. In friendships with our brothers and sisters in Christ, we find people who will rejoice with us in the good times and cry with us when our worlds fall apart.

Fellowship rubs off our apathy and complacency. At times, we need a fellow Christian to challenge us spiritually. Perhaps, we have lost our excitement in following God and we require someone to remind us to get back to the basics of attending worship and spending time in God's Word. Maybe our faith growth has stalled and a push from a caring friend is necessary for stepping out in trust. Or we've slid into some bad habits and destructive attitudes and we need a courageous sister in Christ to point us back to the right path.

Fellowship rubs off our pride and self-importance. Often this nail file appears in the form of the person who simply rubs us the wrong way. The person who intentionally hurts us. Someone whose personality we find annoying. God often uses these people to hone our patience and sharpen our ability to offer Christlike grace. Difficult people offer us opportunities to grow in commitment to the whole Body of Christ, to develop love that gives even when it is not returned, and to grow in trust as we lean on God to provide the grace to be kind. But in order to offer love and grace, we need to lay aside pride. We must let go of our own self-importance to see even challenging people as a vital part of the Body of Christ.

I pray you will find brothers and sisters in Christ who will smooth off the rough edges of your life. Fellow believers who will help erase the heart-breaking losses of living on this earth. People who inspire you and cheer you on as you run the race of faith.

And I pray that as you encounter those people who challenge your patience, you will look at them as opportunities to grow in love and kindness. To view them as chances to develop a dependence on God for the extra grace required. To see them as instruments in God's sharpening tool box.

God of grace, thank You for the gift of fellowship. I don't know what I would do without the support of my brothers and sisters in Christ. Help me to be an encouragement to my fellow believers. Give me Your grace when I encounter people I find difficult to love. In Jesus' name. Amen.

Day Four

Soul Study

1. Proverbs 27:17 says, "Iron sharpens iron, and one man sharpens another." When have you encountered these sharpening effects of fellowship? Write about your experience in one or two of these refining processes.

   Fellowship rubs off our sadness and isolation.

   Fellowship rubs off our apathy and complacency.

   Fellowship rubs off our pride and self-importance.

2. What do you think are some barriers to true fellowship?

3. Colossians 3:12–17 gives detailed instructions on living in fellowship with God's people. Read the passage and use the SACRED reading process we discovered in Week 2 to listen to God's Word.

> **Silence your thoughts.** (Allow your mind to quiet down.)
>
> **Attend to the passage.** (Read the passage out loud, pausing when the Spirit brings a part of it to your attention.)
>
> **Contemplate the Word.** (Meditate on the passage, asking, "How does this passage speak to my life?")
>
> **Respond to the text.** (Pray, pouring out your heart to God in response to what you have read.)
>
> **Exhale and rest.** (Read the text again and simply rest in the love of God.)
>
> **Dwell in the Word.** (Take a truth or promise with you into your day.)

4. Lord, what truth do You want me to see today?

5. Write out this week's memory verse.

A SOUL GUIDE

*In those days Mary arose and went with haste into the hill country,
to a town in Judah, and she entered the house of Zechariah
and greeted Elizabeth. Luke 1:39—40*

God created us to need the communion of others: communion in the sense of fellowship with one another; communion in the sense of sharing thoughts and feelings.

We see this even at the beginning of creation. God created Eve because, as He said, "It is not good for man to be alone."

Let me paraphrase this a little and add, "It is especially not good for woman to be alone."

Are you with me here? I mean, I look at my husband and, at times, he seems perfectly happy to be alone—with the communion of his big-screen TV and remote, of course.

But we women, we need other women. We need other women to give us courage when we're afraid, to give us a hand to hold when we're lonely, a shoulder to cry on when our hearts are torn apart. We need other women to remind us God is faithful and to help us accept His plan for our lives. We need other women to guide us on the spiritual path God has mapped out for us.

God knows this. We can see this in the story of Mary and Elizabeth. Right after Gabriel told Mary she would give birth to the Son of God, He told her:

> And behold, your relative Elizabeth in her old age has also
> conceived a son, and this is the sixth month with her who
> was called barren. Luke 1:36

Don't you love it? God realized Mary would need someone to mentor and encourage her. So He provided Elizabeth. Elizabeth was the perfect mentor for Mary. She was older and wiser. She was just a few months further along in the pregnancy experience, so she could offer Mary a little advice on how to deal with morning sickness and swollen ankles.

Elizabeth could also be an emotional guide for Mary. As an unwed mother, Mary was certain to become the subject of town chatter. Elizabeth also knew the sting of gossip. We know this because when she discovered she was pregnant, she said, "Thus the Lord has done for me in the days when He looked on me, to take away my reproach among people" (Luke 1:25). Elizabeth would be able give Mary some direction through the minefield of public rumor.

But most important, Elizabeth could act as Mary's soul guide. Both women were experiencing their own miracles. Both women were called to have unique roles in God's redemption plan. But being a part of God's plan wasn't always going to be easy. Mary would require encouragement to trust the heavenly Father's design for her life.

We all need guides for this life. We find them in the form of pastors who lead us to deeper faith and teachers who guide us to a deeper understanding of God's Word. But at times, we may realize we need a more personal soul guide—a person who listens to our specific challenges and shares in the nitty-gritty of life. We may find this soul guide in the form of a mentor or an accountability partner.

A mentor is usually someone a little older or a little farther down the path we want to take. When we first moved to Aurora, Illinois, I had some difficulty with one of the members of the congregation. I didn't how to handle it, but I did know another pastor's wife in town. I respected this woman who had just a few more years in ministry than I did. I asked if I could meet with her and pick her brain about this sticky situation. She graciously agreed and, through her advice, I was able to handle the problem. After the initial problem was resolved, we continued to meet about once a month to talk and share prayer requests. Bea was my soul guide through one part of my life path.

While a mentor is usually someone older and more experienced, an accountability partner is a spiritual peer. Accountability partners agree to come together periodically to pray for each other and to speak openly about their struggles. They challenge each other to keep their commitments to God and to the people in their lives.

I'm thankful that God has placed two people in my life that I consider accountability partners. Both Gail and Linda challenge me spiritually and pray for me regularly. I admire the Christian walk of both these women. Most important, I know I can share what God is doing in my life with these friends. I can honestly admit my failures and weaknesses and still be loved.

Whether in the form of a mentor or accountability partner, soul guides are important to spiritual growth. An effective soul guide motivates and empowers. She is willing to listen intently and pray fervently. She shares her own vulnerabilities along with her expertise.

A soul guide is another sharpening tool in God's tool ox. Like a manicure files jagged edges from our nails, a soul guide smooths out life's rough path. She provides guidance when the way seems uncertain. When it is tempting to leave the path, she gently pulls her partner back to the way of life.

God may not send Gabriel to your house to tell you who your perfect mentor is or who the ideal accountability partner will be, but just as He did for Mary, God provides the right people in our lives to help us on our journey. He will provide someone like Elizabeth—someone who has a strong commitment to God and believes His Word. Trust God to provide a sister in Christ to walk with you in your journey of faith.

Ask God to provide the soul guide you need.

Holy Spirit, thank You for being the ultimate Soul Guide. I am grateful for the people You have placed in my life who have helped me along the path of life. Show me who would be a wise soul guide for this portion of my earthly trek. Help me to lead others as You give me the opportunity. In Jesus' name. Amen.

ON MENTORING

As you consider finding a mentor or being a mentor, consider these things:

☼ When you are looking for a mentor, think about what character qualities you want to develop. Reflect on the type of person you want to be "when you grow up." Then think of who you know that exhibits those qualities.

✵ As a mentee, seek wisdom from an older or more mature person. Invite the mentor to challenge you to grow.

✵ If you are asked to be a mentor, consider it a worthy calling. The Bible encourages older women to "train the young women to love their husbands and children, to be self-controlled, pure, working at home, kind, and submissive to their own husbands, that the word of God may not be reviled" (Titus 2:4–5).

✵ If you see a younger woman you would like to mentor, you can initiate the relationship without making the other woman feel she desperately needs a mentor by simply inviting her to lunch or coffee and developing a relationship.

Day Five

Soul Study

1. Think about people in your life who have acted as soul guides—pastors, teachers, mentors, accountability partners, and close Christian friends. List their names and write a prayer of thanks for the people who have supported you in your Christian journey.

2. If you sense the need for an accountability partner or mentor in your life, begin with prayer. Ask God to bring someone to mind. When the Holy Spirit offers a name, approach the person with your request. If she agrees to the relationship, arrange for a meeting and discuss the following:

   How often you will meet

   Specific challenges for which you desire guidance

   Areas of growth you want to concentrate on

3. Read Luke 1:26–56.

   a. Put yourself in Mary's shoes. Describe the feelings you might have experienced when Gabriel showed up at your house.

   b. Reread verse 36. How might have these angelic words comforted you?

   c. How did Elizabeth know Mary was pregnant with the Savior (vv. 41–45)?

   d. If you were Mary, how might have Elizabeth's words have encouraged you?

   e. How can you use the example of Mary and Elizabeth's relationship to seek out a soul guide or to act as a soul guide?

4. Lord, what truth do You want me to see today?

5. Write out this week's memory verse.

Group Activities

1. Give one another manicures. Ask everyone to bring their favorite shades of polish and serve one another by making everyone's hands pretty.

2. Discuss the week's readings and Soul Studies. Allow each woman to choose one question that speaks to her heart. After she gives her answer, open up that question to the other members of the group. Ask some of the women to share their experience with the Spa Session activities from page 155.

3. God has designed us to live in community. Plan either a time of fellowship or service for your group. Here are some ideas:

   Fellowship ideas: potluck meal, meeting at a restaurant for a girl's night out, game night, or ice cream buffet (everyone brings a carton of ice cream, syrup, or topping).

   Service ideas: volunteer at a women's shelter in your community, do a 5K walk together for a charity, write and send cards to the sick and shut-ins in your church, send Christmas cards or gifts to servicemen from your congregation.

4. Close in prayer.

PRAY: CALL UPON GOD

Breathing

Something as simple as breathing can become a multifaceted topic at the spa. The massage therapist may give her client specific breathing instructions as she works on the muscles. In a session on reducing stress, a life coach may teach calming breathing methods. The Pilates instructor tells the women in her class when to inhale and exhale with every core-strengthening movement.

Breathing is a necessary function of the body—without it, we wouldn't last long. Prayer is essential to our souls. Just as inhaling floods our cells with oxygen, prayerfully spending time in God's Word fills us with His love. Exhaling releases carbon dioxide and other toxins. Breathing out our sorrows and dilemmas releases them to God. Through prayer, our empty souls receive what God longs to give us in His Word.

The Spirit breathes God's grace into us through the Word and we breathe out our prayers and petitions.

> To be a Christian without prayer is no more possible than to be alive without breathing.
>
> Martin Luther[37]

MEMORY VERSE

Lord, teach us to pray. Luke 11:1

Day One

WATCH AND PRAY

Watch and pray that you may not enter into temptation.
Matthew 26:41

We had been here before, but it never felt like this. Every night this week, we visited this quiet garden. But tonight the stillness was unnerving instead of peaceful. Every twig that snapped startled me. Every rustle in the leaves made me turn around.

Even Jesus seemed tense. When we reached our usual spot, He said, "My soul is overwhelmed with sorrow. Stay here and pray with Me. Pray that you will not fall into temptation."

I lowered myself to the ground and leaned against one of the ancient olive trees, its bark rough against my back. I watched as the Lord walked a few steps and fell—face to the ground. I couldn't hear His words, yet it was clear He was in anguish. Sweat poured down a face contorted in agony.

As I saw Jesus wrestling in prayer, I remembered His instruction to us. I began to pray. But it had been a long day. The wine we drank at dinner was making me sleepy.

The next thing I knew Jesus was standing over us, asking why we couldn't pray for just one hour. I asked myself the same question. It was clear our Leader was dealing with a horrendous burden. His only request was prayer. *Why couldn't I keep my eyes open and perform this simple task?*

Once again, Jesus went away to pray. If anything, His prayers were more earnest. It was excruciating to watch. I turned away. The overwhelming sadness of the night was more than I could bear.

It seemed only a moment before Jesus' words woke me once again, "Are you still sleeping? Wake up! The time has come."

It is painful to read about Jesus' time in Gethsemane. Picturing my Savior face down on the ground, pleading for a different way to save me, is heartbreaking. My soul is overwhelmed when I contemplate the anguish He went through in the olive grove.

Yet Jesus' example of prayer teaches us to pray. The Gospels tell us Jesus prayed at all the important points of His ministry. He spoke to His Father at His Baptism. He spent the night in prayer before He chose the twelve apostles. Jesus often rose early in the morning to spend time alone with the Father. And now, here, before His greatest work, Jesus spent time in prayer. Examining this time in the Garden of Gethsemane can teach us about prayer.

Prayer expresses our openness to God. Jesus was open about the anguish He felt. He told His closest disciples, "My soul is very sorrowful, even to death" (Matthew 26:38). His natural reaction to the sorrow was to go to His Father: "If it be possible, let this cup pass from Me" (Matthew 26:39). Since God commands us to pray and promises to hear us, we can confidently bare our souls to Him in honest communication. In fact, God wants nothing more than for us to come to Him with our needs and wants. We can be like Jesus and pour out our heartfelt desires.

Prayer calls in faith to the One who can align our hearts to His will. Jesus didn't stop with His deep-felt request. He continued, "Nevertheless, not as I will, but as You will" (Matthew 26:39). Although Jesus prayed for a different path than the cross, He was willing to go through with it, if it was the Father's will. Jesus' prayer shows us that we can pray for anything, but our greatest desire should be for God's will.

God's "good and acceptable and perfect" will is always best (Romans 12:2). But my stubborn belief that I know better often prevents me from wholeheartedly believing that truth. Sometimes I am unable to honestly pray "Not as I will, but as You will." It's then I begin with the prayer "Lord, I cannot say I want Your will, but I *want* to want Your will. Deep down I know that Your way is best. Work in my heart to desire and trust Your perfect will in this situation."

Prayer demonstrates our union with other believers. Even Jesus wanted His close friends to pray with Him. All of the apostles came to the garden, but He asked His three closest companions to come nearer. In the Lord's Prayer, Jesus taught us to pray to *our* Father. When we are struggling, uniting in prayer with our brothers and sisters in Christ may strengthen our frail souls.

Prayer pleads to the One who gives us strength. Jesus gave specific instruction to Peter, James, and John: "Watch and pray that you may not enter into temptation" (Matthew 26:41). Jesus knew a time of great testing was coming for these men. Soon they would witness their Teacher's death. Connecting to God in prayer would give them access to the greatest power in the universe. I admit I don't often approach God in prayer with this purpose. I don't realize that my safety and protection come from prayer. I am too weak to battle Satan on my own.[38] Jesus' instructions to His disciples make me realize prayer to resist temptation should be a greater priority.

Jesus earnestly prayed that the cup of suffering would be taken away, but the sacrifice of the perfect Son of God was the only way to save mankind. Father, Son, and Spirit put their omniscient heads together and could not come up with a different way. So Jesus did not receive a yes answer to His urgent plea, but He did receive support. Luke 22:43 tells us, "There appeared to Him an angel from heaven, strengthening Him." We may not receive the answer we desire when we pray, but God will give us the power to keep going when the answer is no.

This week, remember Jesus' example in prayer. As you spend time with our gracious Father, ask that your heart be aligned to His will. Enlist the prayer support of others. Pray for the strength to battle daily temptation. Watch in anticipation of God's answer—granting your requests or supplying strength.

Breathe out the sorrows of your soul. Breathe in the grace the Spirit gives through God's Word.

Holy Savior, my heart breaks at the agony of soul You went through for me. Work in me the same desire for the Father's will that You always displayed. Thank You for Your gifts of honest prayer and extravagant grace. In Your name. Amen.

Soul Study

1. Picture yourself as one of Jesus' three closest disciples. Describe your emotions as you watched Jesus praying in the Garden of Gethsemane.

2. Read the three accounts of Jesus' prayer in Gethsemane: Matthew 26:36–46; Mark 14:32–42; and Luke 22:39–46.
   a. This story is probably familiar to you. What new insights did you observe by reading the three accounts together?

   b. What did you learn about prayer from Jesus' example? How will this change the way you pray?

   c. Jesus prayed to His Father, "Yet not what I will, but what You will" (Mark 14:36). What sometimes prevents you from praying that same prayer?

d. Jesus told His disciples, "Watch and pray that you may not enter into temptation. The spirit indeed is willing, but the flesh is weak" (Matthew 26:41). How can "watching" help us avoid temptation?

How can praying help us avoid temptation?

e. The disciples struggled to follow Christ's instruction to pray. How do you relate to their experience?

3. Lord, what truth do You want me to see today?

4. Write out this week's memory verse.

Spa Session

Prayer is a lifeline for our souls. Prayer is probably not new to you. You pray in church. You pray at home. This week, try an experience in prayer you haven't tried before. Here are a few ideas:

⚙ Use a prayer journal to write out your prayers every day this week. I find this method especially useful when I struggle to keep my mind focused. Keeping pen to paper also keeps my mind from wandering.

⚙ Look into using a prayer app. Two to try: Echo Prayer Manager (https://new.echoprayer.com/) is designed to help you "pray without ceasing" (1 Thessalonians 5:17) by sending you prayer reminders on your phone. Pray Now (http://www.cph.org/p-18058-pray-now-app .aspx) offers a disciplined order of daily prayer centered in Scripture.

⚙ Make a prayer collage of pictures for your refrigerator, bulletin board, or computer screen. Post pictures of the people and concerns on your prayer list. For instance, find pictures of your loved ones, cut out a piece of the classified ads to symbolize the job someone is searching for, or use a picture of a bubbling brook to represent peace.

⚙ Pray a Palms Up, Palms Down Centering Prayer. Place your palms down on your lap as you spill out all your worries, doubts, and fears to God. Let them fall out of your hands. Then turn your palms up, symbolizing patient expectation of receiving from God. Meditate on His words of forgiveness, encouragement, and love in the Gospel.

⚙ Experience a fast. Read about fasting in Day Three and try a fast. If medically able, try a food fast or partial fast. Other options include abstaining from shopping or media for a time. Journal about your experience—how did it change you and your relationship with God?

Day Two

SOUL OXYGEN

Pray without ceasing. 1 Thessalonians 5:17

Did you know that something as simple as breathing can reduce the tension that strangles our lives? Medical research shows focused breathing for twenty minutes a day can diminish anxiety and pressure. Deep breathing boosts the flow of oxygen to your brain and stimulates the parasympathetic nervous system, promoting a state of peace. Focusing on your breathing keeps you in the moment and temporarily diverts your attention from your problems and worries.[39]

During my visit to the spa, it seemed everyone on the staff had instructions for breathing. The Pilates instructor gave us specific breathing instructions for each exercise. A life coach talked about lessening stress through breathing methods. The cardio kickboxing instructor yelled, "Don't forget to breathe!"

All this talk about breathing made me remember: Prayer is as necessary to our souls as the air we breathe is to our bodies. Martin Luther wrote, "To be a Christian without prayer is no more possible than to be alive without breathing."[40] Prayer is receiving the oxygen our souls need to survive. We exhale our sorrows and worries and inhale God's grace through His Word. We breathe out our confessions and failures and breathe in Christ's promise of forgiveness.

The Father knows we need the oxygen of prayer, and so He invites us to pray. He tells us, "Call upon Me in the day of trouble" (Psalm 50:15). God has given us a direct line to His throne room with unlimited minutes. He desires nothing less than we come to Him with all of our dilemmas, crises, and predicaments.

Prayer is so necessary that God even commands us to pray. First Thessalonians tells us, "Pray without ceasing" (5:17). Our habit of prayer is to be as continuous as breathing. We rarely think about moving air in and out of our lungs. While intentionally paying attention to breathing can bring health benefits to our bodies and minds, God designed our bodies to constantly inhale oxygen and exhale carbon dioxide automatically. I would like to make continual prayer just as real in my life. How can I make keeping in contact with my heavenly Father my default mode of operation?

I admit I struggle with this command to pray without ceasing. Many times I start the day with the intent to connect with God moment by moment, only to tumble into bed at day's end realizing that I have not given Him much thought since my morning devotions. I recognized the fact that I needed more. Just as our bodies cannot exist on one breath in the morning and one breath before we go to bed, our souls can wilt when we try to survive on a twice-a-day prayer regimen. But how could I begin to "pray without ceasing"?

I started to make some progress a few years ago when I realized that when I'm worried about something, I constantly think about it. The problem simply hijacks my thought process. What if I turned every anxious thought into a prayer? It wouldn't be long and I would be praying continually!

This worked so well that I began to look for other ways to turn thoughts into prayers. Next, I used the same technique with short-as-a-breath prayers of thanksgiving. Instead of simply thinking, "Wow, look at that blazing-red maple tree!" I also shot up a quick prayer, thanking God for the beauty of His creation. After talking with a close friend over the phone, I offered a short prayer of gratitude for her support.

Lately, I've added quick-as-a-breath prayers in the form of intercession. Often my life is crazy busy and I don't get to see my friends and family as often as I'd like. When a specific person would come to mind, I'd feel guilty I hadn't taken the time to connect with her. But wallowing in guilt doesn't do any good, so now I convert the remorse into a petition for their welfare. After all, perhaps God brought that person to mind because she needed prayer in that moment.

And just the other night at our Wednesday night Bible study, my friend Pam suggested we try this technique with confession. Instead of "saving up" all of her confessing for her nightly prayers, she thought of how freeing it would be to repent in the moment. If we exhale, acknowledging our sin and shortcomings, we can then inhale, receiving Christ's promise of forgiveness. The rest of the day we can be free from carrying the burden of our wrongdoing.

We can confidently inhale the promise that God hears us, and then exhale our prayer requests. The prophet Zechariah wrote God's assurance, "They will call upon My name, and I will answer them" (Zechariah 13:9). King David was confident God was listening to his prayers: "The LORD has heard my plea; the LORD accepts my prayer" (Psalm 6:9). Jesus promised, "Ask, and you will receive, that your joy may be full" (John 16:24). Although on earth we will never reach perfection in praying without ceasing, we can grow in trust that the Father is always ready to listen. Our prayers never go to voicemail.

Just as we can do nothing physically without breathing, we can do nothing spiritually without Jesus. Breathe in your Savior's name and breathe out a desperate prayer for grace. Receive what you need in the moment.

Like the kickboxing instructor at the spa, I'm telling you, "Don't forget to breathe!" With every breath, release your worries to the Almighty. Offer up sacrifices of thanksgiving throughout the day. When a friend or family member comes to mind, silently exhale a petition to the God who cares. Inhale His gracious promises.

Dear heavenly Father, thank You that You have given me a direct line to Your throne. I am so grateful that I can always call to You. Help me to make continual prayer a habit in my life as I exhale my worries and concerns and inhale Your grace through Your Word. In Jesus' name. Amen.

Soul Study

1. Sit quietly and observe your breath. Use a timer or watch with a second hand and count how many breaths you take in a minute. Next, do some jumping jacks or run in place for a couple of minutes. Again, count how many times you breathe in one minute. Was there a difference? What does this tell you about your body's need for air? How does this apply to our need for prayer?

2. God promises to hear our prayers. His words of grace and assurance are oxygen to our souls. Write out the following promises.
   a. Isaiah 65:24

   b. Jeremiah 33:3

   c. John 16:24

   d. 1 John 5:14

   Circle the promise that means the most to you today. Why does that one touch your heart?

   Write that promise on a card and carry it with you. Today as you breathe out your concerns, thanksgivings, and confessions, remind yourself of God's constant supply of grace.

3. Luke 18:1–8 relates Jesus' parable about prayer. What does Jesus teach us about prayer? What does He teach about the Father? How is the Father different from the unrighteous judge? Read the passage and use the SACRED reading process to listen to God's Word to you. Perhaps imagine yourself as the widow who comes to the judge.

Silence your thoughts. (Allow your mind to quiet down.)

Attend to the passage. (Read the passage out loud, pausing when the Spirit brings a part of it to your attention.)

Contemplate the Word. (Meditate on the passage, asking, "How does this passage speak to my life?")

Respond to the text. (Pray, pouring out your heart to God in response to what you have read.)

Exhale and rest. (Read the text again and simply rest in the love of God.)

Dwell in the Word. (Take a truth or promise with you into your day.)

4. Lord, what truth do You want me to see today?

5. Write out this week's memory verse.

Day Three

FASTING

*"Yet even now," declares the L*ORD*, "return to Me with all your heart, with fasting, with weeping, and with mourning." Joel 2:12*

My stomach growled.

I was about to get out of my chair to get a snack when I remembered: *Not today. I'm fasting. Stomach, you'll just have to rumble.*

I have not fasted often. In fact, until a few years ago, I had never fasted from food. Frankly, I like my breakfast, lunch, and dinner. I also enjoy a morning snack, an afternoon nibble, and a little evening nosh. I wasn't sure I could give up food—even for a limited period of time.

But several times in my life, I have felt the need to fast. To wean myself from drawing strength from earthly resources. To draw from the everlasting supply of power.

I first practiced the discipline of fasting when I was faced with an important task I did not feel qualified to accomplish. In fasting, I acknowledged my weakness and my need for God's strength to complete the job. Every time my stomach growled, I was reminded of my humanness. Every rumble in the belly gave me cause to turn to God for His sustaining power.

In abstaining from food, I remember that I live in a frail body that cannot be sustained without God's provision. Prayer, combined with fasting, helps me approach God as His helpless and vulnerable child. I breathe out my usual self-reliance and breathe in dependence on my Father's mercy and strength.

Fasting helps us notice our souls. At a spa, you can retreat from the world for a time to take care of your body. You abandon your usual routine to concentrate on your health. Through fasting, we withdraw from our outward preoccupations in order to pay attention to our inner needs. We relinquish a physical appetite, desire, or comfort in order to make more room for God. Fasting helps us to release the grip the material world has on us. As we temporarily ignore the desires of our bodies, we can better hear the yearnings of our soul.

Jesus fasted before He began His earthly ministry. The recorded story of His wilderness experience reminds us we cannot truly be satisfied by material comforts. The Book of Matthew tells us, "After fasting forty days and forty nights, He was hungry" (4:2). (Possibly the biggest understatement in Scripture.) Yet when Satan tempted Jesus to turn stones into bread, Jesus answered, "It is written, 'Man shall not live by bread alone, but by every word that comes from the mouth of God'" (Matthew 4:4). Jesus' words remind us that although food may fill a growling stomach, it doesn't feed our souls. God alone can satisfy our spiritual hunger.

Fasting is not always abstaining from all food. During Lent, I have observed partial fasts. In a small way, denying myself chocolate or ice cream for forty days reminds me of Jesus' sacrifice. Sometimes fasting is not even about the stuff we put in our mouths. One year our family gave up television for the forty days before Easter. Another Lenten season I renounced shopping—going only to the grocery store or pharmacy for essentials. (We saved a lot of money that year.)

If you've never fasted before, but would like to try, here are a few ideas:

☼ Remember to check with a doctor before abstaining from food. Fasting may not be recommended for individuals with certain medical conditions.

☼ Try a twenty-four hour fast. Begin after supper one day and don't eat until the following day's evening meal. That way you skip only two meals. Use the time you would have used eating to feed your soul. Connect with God through prayer and Scripture.

☼ Observe a partial fast. Abstain from a favorite treat like coffee or chocolate for a specified period of time. Every time a desire for that treat surfaces, use it as a reminder to turn to the Father.

☼ Fast from media. Give up television or the Internet for a day or a week. Instead of spending your time on media, read God's Word and other uplifting books.

☼ Declare a shopping fast. Only go to stores to purchase essentials. Realize how little you require. Turn to God—the source of all we need.

A spa offers the opportunity to get away from the stress of everyday life. Shutting out the rest of the world for a time enables us to attend to the needs of our bodies. At the Soul Spa, we can use fasting as a means to focus on the neediness of our spirits. Shut out the rumblings of a stomach, the desire to shop, the dependence on technology—for a time. Listen to the cravings of your heart. Realize the Bread of Life is the only one who can satisfy a starving soul.

Bread of Life, hear the yearnings of my hungry spirit. Show me when I need to use the discipline of fasting to observe the needs of my soul or to draw from Your strength. May this time of abstaining from worldly comforts remind me that You are the only one who truly satisfies. In Jesus' name. Amen.

Day Three

Soul Study

1. Have you ever observed a fast? Write about what you abstained from and for how long. How did the experience change you?

2. Read Joel 2:12–17. The prophet Joel wrote about a devastating locust plague that he viewed as a foretaste of the judgment of God.
   a. Why did Joel encourage the people to fast (v. 17)?

   b. What would fasting demonstrate (v. 12)?

c. Verse 13 says, "Rend your hearts and not your garments." Ripping one's clothes was a gesture of great remorse. But God tells them to rend their hearts instead. How could fasting demonstrate our frailty? How can this frailty lead to heart change?

d. List some of the characteristics of God that Joel mentioned in verse 13.

e. How can these characteristics help us when we decide to fast?

f. In verses 15–17, Joel declares a national fast. If you were to fast with a group of people for a united purpose, what would that purpose be?

3. Lord, what truth do You want me to see today?

4. Write out this week's memory verse.

Day Four

INTERCESSION

First of all, then, I urge that supplications, prayers, intercessions, and thanksgivings be made for all people. 1 Timothy 2:1

"I wish I could do something to help you! But at least I can pray."

Have you ever said something similar to someone? Someone experiencing loss? Or pain? Or tragedy? In our culture of doing, we want to act. We desperately want to ease the pain. But sometimes, there seems to be nothing we can *do*. The illness is serious. Our friend lives hundreds of miles away. Our own financial situation prevents us from sending money. We feel powerless and so we say, "At least I can pray."

Think about that a minute. Is prayer the *least* thing I can do? Or is it the greatest? The assistance I can offer is puny at best. Even my best help is often flawed and insufficient. But when I *pray*, I am calling on the power of the almighty God. When I *pray*, I'm enlisting support that is effective and unlimited. When I *pray*, God comes to the rescue with exactly what is needed.

Intercession is defined as "a prayer to God on behalf of another."[41] We breathe in the hurts and pain of others and breathe out a prayer to the One who can heal the hurt and soothe the pain.

When someone we love is ill or in desperate circumstances, we do not need to be reminded to pray for that person. We become the centurion pleading for his paralyzed servant (Matthew 8:5–6). We act the part of the Canaanite woman begging for a few crumbs of blessing for her daughter (Matthew 15:21–28). We bang on heaven's door, imploring God's mercy.

But the Bible instructs us not to stop with people we know. The apostle Paul urged Timothy:

> First of all, then, I urge that supplications, prayers, intercessions, and thanksgivings be made for all people, for kings and all who are in high positions, that we may lead a peaceful and quiet life, godly and dignified in every way. This is good, and it is pleasing

in the sight of God our Savior, who desires all people to be saved and to come to the knowledge of the truth. 1 Timothy 2:1–4

We are to pray for all people. Paul specifically mentions kings and people in authority. As I write this chapter, we are nearing a national election. Here in Illinois, political ads are running nonstop. My usual reaction is exasperation with the attacking messages on my television. But what if I used these incessant commercials as a reminder to pray? Instead of complaining, I can pray for government officials. I can plead God's will would be accomplished in the voting booths.

Paul also reminds us that God desires all people to be saved. Who in my life doesn't yet know Christ? Do I pray for them regularly? I forget what a privilege it is to approach the eternal God on behalf of a friend. But I need to pray. Pray the Holy Spirit would start a spark of faith in her heart. Pray I would be courageous enough to share how Christ has changed my life.

How do we intercede? I'm learning that intercession should begin with the prayer that never fails, "Thy will be done." I'm tempted to come to God with my plan for the lives of my loved ones and demand He rubber-stamp it. Give Carla a job in town so she doesn't move away. Find Heather a husband—soon. But I need to remember God's will is always best. So I pray for the Father's perfect plan. I ask that He show me how to pray for this need.

I am thankful that when I don't have a clue how to pray, the Holy Spirit is willing to step in. Romans 8:26 assures us that when we don't know how to pray, "the Spirit Himself intercedes for us with groanings too deep for words." He "arranges the words and form of prayer for us. He places them on our lips for how and what we should pray."[42] We whisper the name of the person on our hearts and the Comforter fills in the blanks.

Even as we pray for others, we are changed. Intercession can be a discipline for our own spiritual transformation because it is an opportunity to grow in trust. Jesus commended the intercessors in the Bible for their faith. He said of the centurion, "With no one in Israel have I found such faith" (Matthew 8:10). He told the Canaanite woman, "O woman, great is your faith!" (Matthew 15:28). Although we hate waiting for the answers to prayers, waiting is an opportunity to develop deeper trust in God's goodness.

Prayer for our loved ones grows our relationship with God because it brings us to our knees again and again. I've never prayed as fervently as when my children were experiencing serious illnesses or desperate job situations. Sorry to say, my prayer life is strongest when I'm begging God to intervene in a life crisis. I become the persistent widow coming again and again to plead my case (Luke 18:1–5). And one thing I've noticed in those times. While the rest of my life looks like it's falling apart, my relationship with God becomes rock solid.

In intercession, we call on the power of the Almighty for the needs of others. We learn to pray for God's will in their lives. We come again and again to plead at the foot of God's throne.

When we pray for others, we don't do the least we can do. Intercession is the greatest thing we can do for those in need.

Heavenly Father, forgive me when I forget prayer is a powerful gift You have given us. May I help others where I can, but never forget prayer is the most important thing I can do for the people in my life. In Jesus' name. Amen.

Day Four

Soul Study

1. What is your biggest struggle in intercessory prayer?

2. How has praying for others increased your own faith?

3. Ephesians 3:14–21 is one of Paul's most eloquent intercessory prayers. Read the passage and answer the following questions.

a. What are your most common requests for the people you pray for?

b. How can this model prayer change the way you intercede for others?

c. List the blessings Paul requested for the people of Ephesus.

i.

ii.

iii.

iv.

v.

vi.

d. Whom do you know who needs the blessings mentioned in Paul's prayer? Write a name by each item you listed above. Take a few minutes to intercede for these brothers and sisters in Christ.

4. Lord, what truth do You want me to see today?

5. Write out this week's memory verse.

Day Five

PRAYING SCRIPTURE

Lord, teach us to pray. Luke 11:1

"Lord, teach us to pray."

This was the fervent request of the disciples after they watched their Teacher pray. Although they probably grew up praying in their Jewish homes, they realized their prayers were lacking.

Like the disciples, I realize my prayer life is deficient. Honestly, I struggle with prayer. Bible study comes naturally to me. I love to open Scripture and hear God speak. But prayer? Prayer sometimes seems nebulous. My mind wanders. I get discouraged when my pleas seem to fall short of heaven.

But I know prayer is a lifeline to God's mercy. I can't ignore it. So I continue to ask, "Lord, teach me to pray."

One of the methods that has breathed life into my frail prayers is praying Scripture. Since Bible study has always been an important part of my relationship with God, using Scripture as the foundation of my prayers has helped my prayer life grow and develop.

When we pray the words of the Bible, we are using God's language. His words have power. They are "spirit and life" (John 6:63). Our own words are limited, but God promises, "My word . . . that goes out from My mouth . . . shall not return to Me empty, but it shall accomplish that which I purpose, and shall succeed in the thing for which I sent it" (Isaiah 55:11). God is at work in the words of Scripture. Using them in my petitions calls on His unlimited potential to work in my life and the lives of the ones I love.

Here are some ways to use God's own words as a guide for your prayers.

Pray the Lord's Prayer. Jesus answered the disciples' request for a prayer lesson by giving them a short and eloquent prayer. It's easy to unconsciously rattle off the well-known words of the Lord's Prayer. But what if I mindfully repeated the words? What if I paused after each phrase, personalizing it to my life?

Our Father who art in heaven. Hallowed by Your name. *Thank You that You are my Father—a perfect caring and loving Father. I confess I am usually much more concerned about bringing recognition to my name. Help me to live to bring glory to Your name.*

Your kingdom come. *Father, You are my King, yet I often live as if I were the ruler of my life. Teach me to live under Your loving rule.*

Using Jesus' own prayer guides our conversation with God. His model teaches us how to pray.

Pray Paul's prayers of intercession. The apostle Paul's epistles include some eloquent prayers for others. One of my favorite Scriptures to pray for the people in my life is Ephesians 1:16–18. As I pray, I insert the name of the person I am praying for wherever there is a "you" or "your."

> I do not cease to give thanks for _____, remembering
> _____ in my prayers, that the God of our Lord Jesus Christ,
> the Father of glory, may give _____ the Spirit of wisdom
> and of revelation in the knowledge of Him, having the eyes of
> _____ hearts enlightened, that _____ may
> know what is the hope to which He has called _____,
> what are the riches of His glorious inheritance in the saints.

Pray the Psalms. When we don't know how to pray, we can turn to the Book of Psalms—the prayer book of the Bible. David and the other psalmists penned authentic prayers for every occasion. Psalm 51 is a transparent prayer of confession: "Have mercy on me, O God, according to Your steadfast love. . . . Against You, You only, have I sinned and done what is evil in Your sight" (vv. 1, 4). Psalm 150 is a boisterous psalm of praise: "Praise Him with sounding cymbals; praise Him with loud clashing cymbals!" (v. 5). An urgent prayer of supplication is found in Psalm 88: "But I, O LORD, cry to You; in the morning my prayer comes before You" (v. 13).

Pray in response to lessons gleaned from God's Word. The words of Scripture guide my prayers as the Holy Spirit teaches me. Whenever the Spirit uses His holy highlighter to bring some of God's Word to my attention, I journal the lessons I learn from Him and respond with an honest prayer. For instance, I recently read Hebrews 12:1 in my morning devotions:

> Therefore, since we are surrounded by so great a cloud of witnesses,
> let us also lay aside every weight, and sin which clings so closely,
> and let us run with endurance the race that is set before us.

Suddenly, I realized that I had been carrying around the heavy burden of trying to do something important for God. Intellectually, I knew God did not require this of me. My head knew there was nothing I could do to make God love me more—or less. But my heart didn't believe I had worth without accomplishments. Viewing this as a burden suddenly made a lot of sense. I wrote this prayer in my journal: "Lord, show me all the weights I have been carrying that slow me down. I want to live lightly in Your love. Take the burden of trying to be 'somebody' and help me realize that I am already loved and honored in Your sight."

Dietrich Bonhoeffer wrote, "The richness of the Word of God ought to determine our prayer, not the poverty of our heart."[43] Praying Scripture aligns our hearts with the heart of God. It's easy to approach God with a laundry list of concerns. Using God's own words to form our prayers helps us discover the desires God has for us. We breathe in the words of our gracious God and breathe them out again as words of petition and praise.

"Lord, teach us to pray." Teach us to pray with Your heart, Your desires, Your words.

Our Father who art in heaven, thank You for the gift of prayer. Through Your Holy Word, teach us to pray. As we come to You, align our hearts with Yours. In Jesus' name we pray. Amen.

PRAYING SCRIPTURE—PASSAGES TO GUIDE YOUR PRAYERS

Prayers of Intercession

| Ephesians 3:14–19 | Philippians 1:9–11 | Colossians 1:9–11 |

Prayers of Adoration

| Psalm 8 | Psalm 96 | Psalm 148 |

Prayers of Confession

| Psalm 6 | Psalm 32 | Psalm 51 |

Prayers of Thanksgiving

| Psalm 100 | Psalm 105:1–3 | Psalm 136 |

Soul Study

1. How would you describe your prayer life?

2. Read Luke 11:1–13.

   a. What prompted the disciples to ask Jesus to teach them how to pray? What do you imagine they saw in Jesus' prayers that made them want to learn more?

   b. After Jesus taught the disciples a simple prayer, He told them some stories. What about these stories makes you bold enough to pray?

   c. Try personalizing the Lord's Prayer. After each petition, expand the thought. Bring *your* praise and petitions to the Father.

Father, hallowed be Your name

Your kingdom come

Give us each day our daily bread

Forgive us our sins, for we ourselves forgive everyone who is indebted to us

And lead us not into temptation

3. Lord, what truth do You want me to see today?

4. Write out this week's memory verse.

Group Activities

1. Try the exercise in the Day Two Soul Study. Talk about the effect breathing has on physical exercise and the effect physical exertion has on breathing. Compare physical exertion and breathing to soul pains and prayer.

2. Discuss the week's readings and Soul Studies. Allow each woman to choose one question that speaks to her heart. After she gives her answer, open up that question to the other members of the group. Ask some of the women to share their experience with the Spa Session activities from page 182.

3. Engage in a prayer activity together. Here are some ideas:

   Do a prayer walk together. Take a stroll around your neighborhood and pray for the people in each house you pass. If you meet in your church, you could walk around the church, praying for the workers, and sit in the pews, interceding for each person who will sit there to worship.

   Make prayer collages together. Ask everyone to bring pictures of people they want to pray for. Perhaps print up pictures of your group. Provide magazines and fun scrapbook materials available to create beautiful reminders to pray.

   Spend some time in conversational prayer. One person in the group opens with a prayer for a person or concern. Other people follow with a short prayer on the same topic. When everyone has prayed for that concern, continue in the same way with another need.

   Pray with a partner. Hand out index cards to everyone and divide the group into pairs. Each pair finds a quiet corner of the room to talk and share prayer requests. As each person communicates her concerns, her partner writes down them on the index card. After a few minutes of sharing, each pair prays together. Take the cards home to pray for each other during the week. Connect with your prayer partner sometime during the week.

4. Close in prayer together as a large group.

ATTUNE: ALTER YOUR LIFE

Life Coach

Massages. Manicures. Exercise classes. Nutritious food. All of these can be part of the spa experience. A weekend spent at a health resort can fine-tune your body and set you on a path to healthy living.

But what will you do when you get home? How will you continue those healthy habits? That's where a life coach steps in. Luxury spas often offer sessions with a life coach—an adviser to help you set and attain goals for a meaningful life.

During our visit to the Soul Spa, we've visited the rooms of study, worship, and prayer. We've explored solitude, discernment, and service. How can we persevere in these practices? Will we continue to care for our soul?

We need a life coach—someone who will guide us to what our soul needs most and help us make soul care a priority in our lives. We can be thankful that Jesus has already given us a guide in the form of the Holy Spirit. It is His role to lead us to our true path of life. He will renew our souls.

> When peace, like a river, attendeth my way,
> When sorrows like sea billows roll;
> Whatever my lot, Thou hast taught me to say,
> It is well, it is well with my soul.

Horatio G. Spafford

MEMORY VERSE

> Beloved, I pray that all may go well with you and that you may be in good health, as it goes well with your soul.
> 3 John 2

Day One

"FOLLOW ME"

And He said to them,
"Follow Me, and I will make you fishers of men."
Immediately they left their nets and followed Him.
Matthew 4:19—20

I used to be content with life on the Sea of Galilee, sitting in a boat with my brother Simon. A good day meant a catch of fish and a few laughs with my crazy sibling. It wasn't an easy life. It meant long hours mending nets. It meant aching muscles and fingers rubbed raw on the ropes. Sometimes, it meant fishing all night and catching . . . nothing.

But it was a good life.

I was content until I heard about a preacher named John who wore clothing made of camel's hair. They said he ate locusts and wild honey! My curiosity pulled me to the shores of the Jordan River where he was preaching. He talked about repentance and baptized anyone who confessed their sins.

Yet repentance and forgiveness of sins weren't his only topics. He also spoke a message about someone much greater who was coming. John said he was only preparing the way for the One who would baptize, not with water, but with the Holy Spirit.

I was fascinated. A hunger in my heart for more than life in a boat drew me back again and again to hear John speak. So I was there when John saw a man walking by and called out, "Look, the Lamb of God who takes away the sin of the world!"

One of John's other disciples and I decided to follow this "Lamb of God." We were walking behind Him when He turned around and asked, "What do you want?"

What did I want? I hardly knew. I did know I wanted a life of more than fishing. I wanted to do more than sit in a boat and fix nets. But more than anything, I wanted to know this man.

I didn't know how to say all that so I stupidly asked, "Rabbi, where are You staying?"

The Rabbi graciously said, "Come, and you will see."

My friend and I ended up spending the whole day with Him. By the end of our time together, we were convinced: this was the Messiah.

I rushed to tell Simon of our discovery. When I brought my brother to Jesus, the Teacher immediately gave him a new name—Peter.

Although my heart hungered for more, we still had our fishing business. One morning, we pulled our boats up on shore, tired and discouraged. It had been another night of catching nothing.

We were washing our nets when we noticed Jesus. At first, we could hardly see Him. So many people were crowding around Him. When Jesus spotted us, He got into our boat and asked Simon to put out a little from shore. He continued to speak to the crowd—while having a little room to breathe.

After Jesus finished His message, He told Simon, "Put out into deeper water, and let down the nets."

Simon looked at me and back to Jesus. "Sir, with all due respect, we've worked all night and haven't caught a thing. But because You say so, I will let down the nets."

No sooner had the nets entered the water than they filled with fish. When we started to pull them out, the nets actually began to break. Quickly, our partners James and John came to help. Soon silvery fish were flailing and flapping around the bottom of both boats.

And that's the last time we went fishing for a long time. Although that kind of success might make a man want to continue in this job, we took a totally different career path. When we reached the shore, Jesus said, "Come, follow Me and I will make you fishers of men."

Some might call us crazy, but that is exactly what we did. We left a life of simple and honest work for one of uncertainty, hardship, and much travel. But during the past three years, we've witnessed countless miracles and learned heavenly principles. Our minds were opened to understand Scripture. We worshiped in the temple. We listened as Jesus taught in the synagogues. We shared a few fish and a couple of loaves of bread with thousands of people.

Most of all, we spent time with Jesus. We became His friends. He touched my soul and I will never be the same.

Following Jesus changes us. The better we know Him, the more our spirits are transformed. When we spend time with the Savior, we cannot stay the same.

We follow Jesus because our hearts hunger for more than what the world offers. Although we may experience happiness and success in this culture, deep down we know we were made for more. Jesus whispers, "What do you want?" We're not exactly sure, but we know we want what the Savior offers—abundant life.

Christ becomes our Teacher, our Rabbi, our Life Coach. As we spend time with Him, Jesus slowly uncovers the design He has planned for our lives all along. Through His Word, our Life Coach outlines the plan for a healthy, thriving soul.

On the outside, our lives may not look much different. Unlike Andrew and Simon and the other disciples, we may not be called by Jesus to leave our day jobs. (If I had been Andrew, I would have been anxious to leave the smelly fish business too!) But when we hear the Rabbi's call, our hearts leave behind the world of activity and doing to settle in to listen and be blessed.

Through time in God's Word, our souls are fed. In solitude and silence, we are better able to hear our Lord's voice. Our minds and bodies engage in worship, reminding us that God is greater than the world we can see. We practice confession and absolution to uncover the true self that God lovingly created. Hospitality and service become ways to share our lives with others. We open our hearts to God in prayer, placing all our concerns and desires in His hands.

Like Andrew and the rest of the disciples, we experience life transformed. We witness Christ's healing work in our souls. But most of all, as we spend time with Jesus, intimacy with the eternal God living in our hearts deepens. We become His friends.

Holy Lord, thank You for inviting me to follow You. Life will never be the same. My soul hungers for so much more than this world offers. Help me to remember abundant life is only found in You. Amen.

Soul Study

1. After reading the story of Andrew, why do you think he felt drawn to follow John the Baptist and Jesus?

2. Read John 1:35–42; Luke 5:1–11; Mark 1:14–20; and Matthew 4:18–22 (in that order).
   a. In John 1:38, Jesus asked Andrew and his companion, "What are you seeking?" Based on Andrew's actions, how do you think his heart wanted to respond to that question?

   b. What would you answer if Jesus appeared before you bodily and asked the question "What do you want?" Take a moment to contemplate your deepest desires. How do these desires match up to what God desires? Write down your thoughts.

c. In Luke 5:5, Peter protested when Jesus told him to let down the fishing nets. Why did he eventually obey?

d. Is Jesus asking you to do something right now that makes no practical sense? What is it? Support a ministry that is new to you? Help a neighbor who doesn't "deserve" kindness?

e. Luke 5:11 says, "When they had brought their boats to land, they left everything and followed Him." I have always been amazed at the disciples' immediate renouncing of their old life to follow Jesus.
Try to imagine yourself as Andrew, Peter, James, or John. Why do you think they were ready for such a drastic life change?

f. God may not call us to leave our entire way of life to follow Him as He called the disciples to do, but we may need to sacrifice some activities in order to spend more time with Jesus. Ask the Lord to show you if there is anything in your life you need to give up in order to deepen your relationship with Him. Write a prayer here.

3. Lord, what truth do You want me to see today?

4. Write out this week's memory verse.

Spa Session

We are coming to the end of our Soul Spa experience. This week, explore practices that will help you make soul care a habit for life. Try a few of these experiences.

❂ Look back on all of the "Spa Session" sections in this book. Circle the activities you would like to try. Make a list and schedule some of them into your calendar for the coming month.

❂ Read about Rest in Day Three. Set aside an afternoon or an entire day this week to rest. Sleep in late. Eat your favorite breakfast. Plan to do something that renews your love for life: walk in the woods, go window-shopping, or have lunch with a friend. Spend some time with the Lord with a practice that breathes life into your soul: SACRED reading, journaling, or praying God's Word.

❂ Explore the concept of simplicity. Try a shopping fast this week or one of the other simplicity activities on page 221.

❂ Set aside one morning or afternoon this week to meet with your Life Coach. Come up with a Rule of Life using the activities on pages 227–28. Pencil in your next coaching session with the Holy Spirit on next month's calendar.

Day Two

LIFE COACH

When the Spirit of truth comes, He will guide you into all the truth, for He will not speak on His own authority, but whatever He hears He will speak, and He will declare to you the things that are to come. John 16:13

Many luxury spas take a holistic approach to wellness. To help you on your way to a fulfilling life, you might find a message similar to this one on a spa menu:

BOOK A LIFE COACHING SESSION

> On your journey to wellness, it is helpful to have a guide. While at our spa, book a session with a personal life coach who will bring out the best possible you. In a one-on-one session, you will discover what you want most in your life and how to get it. A coach can assist you in setting, meeting, and evaluating goals that will lead you on a purposeful path. Get the clarity and focus you need for your life.

A life coach on staff can help you define exactly what happiness means in your life. This coach will enable you to live out your dreams and design a meaningful life.

A life coach can be very beneficial. If you're like me, it's easy to bumble through life without making any progress. At times, we could all use someone to guide us in setting and achieving goals instead of simply drifting through life.

In our spiritual life, we also need a life coach. We can be thankful that God has already provided a Guide for us in the form of the Holy Spirit. Jesus told His disciples:

> When the Spirit of truth comes, He will guide you into all the truth, for He will not speak on His own authority, but whatever

He hears He will speak, and He will declare to you the things that are to come. John 16:13

The verb for "guide" that Jesus uses is the same word used for guiding a blind person on a road.[44] What an apt comparison. The spiritual road we walk on is an unseen one. We do not yet have spiritual eyes—we need a Guide who does.

A life coach helps her clients clarify what is important to them. But our spiritual Life Coach does much more than that—He guides us into truth. We may think we know what is significant and essential to happiness, but we might be mistaken. The Holy Spirit has eternal and omniscient knowledge on what is truly vital to a joyful life. Through the Word, He directs us to that truth.

A life coach aids her clients in setting purposeful goals. Through the pages of Scripture, the Holy Spirit outlines a plan for abundant life. Step by step, He leads us to the life God has designed for us.

A life coach helps her clients when they begin to lose traction. If their enthusiasm fades, she is there to encourage them and keep them on track. My heavenly Life Coach provides the motivation I need to continue on my ultimate life path. Philippians 2:13 says, "For it is God who works in you, both to will and to work for His good pleasure." The Holy Spirit teaches me how to pursue God's amazing plan for my life *and* gives me the desire to actually follow through.

I imagine a coaching session with the Holy Spirit. Like any good counselor, He would be gifted at asking questions to help me discover more about myself. My Life Coach might begin with a few basic questions: "Do you believe that I will guide you into all truth? Do you trust Me to lead you into that truth even when it may seem we are going the wrong way? Do you understand how much the triune God loves you and wants you to have an amazing life?"

Next, the Holy Spirit might ask a few questions about my life: "Where can your gifts meet the needs of your community and world? Where does your soul need healing? Are you striving to live as your beautifully created self, or are you hiding behind a mask? What sins and failures are you still carrying around? Can you bring them to the cross for forgiveness?"

Finally, my Life Coach might ask about our relationship: "When will you meet with Me? Are you willing to make our time a priority? Can you be patient even if I don't give you all the answers you want right away? Can you follow Me one step at a time?"

After we had discussed these questions, I imagine the Holy Spirit reassuring me that the God of the universe has an amazing plan for my life. I think He would remind me that He is not only a coach but a Comforter who deeply cares about my hurts, fears, and longings. Guiding me through the pages of Scripture, He would show me how to obtain an abundant life step by step. Best of all, He would speak the words of Jesus to me and lead me to a more intimate relationship with my Savior.

A life coach at a spa can be an effective investment, but our spiritual Life Coach is an eternal blessing. He is a gift from Jesus leading us through this earthly existence to life forever with God. This Life Coach actually does possess the ability to bring out the best in us.

Holy Spirit, thank You for being the guide I so desperately need for this life. Help me to trust Your ability to lead me on a path to truth. Heal my soul and empower me to live the life the Father designed for me. In Jesus' name. Amen.

Day Two

Soul Study

1. If you were going to hire a life coach, what three goals might you want her to help you achieve (for example, advance your career, organize your home, and start a new business)?

2. Jesus described the work of the Holy Spirit in John 16:5–15. Read the passage and answer the questions below.

a. What does Jesus call the Holy Spirit in verse 7?

b. The Greek the word there is *paraclete*, which means "one who comes alongside to help." A *paraclete* is an encourager or assistant. In various versions, this word is translated as Comforter, Helper, Counselor, Advocate, and Friend. Which term means the most to you right now? Why?

c. Why did Jesus say the Holy Spirit would convict the world concerning sin (v. 9)?

d. Even after we have saving faith, we daily struggle with unbelief in some areas of our lives. How do you sometimes wrestle with unbelief?

e. John 16:13 says, "When the Spirit of truth comes, He will guide you into all the truth." Imagine you are in a life coaching session with the Holy Spirit and He asks you questions that lead you to truth. Read the following questions. Choose the ones that speak to you and write out your most honest and authentic answers.

Do you believe that I will guide you into all truth?

Do you trust Me to lead you into that truth even when it may seem we are going the wrong way?

Do you understand how much the triune God loves you and wants you to have an amazing life?

Where can your gifts meet the needs of your community and world?

Where does your soul need healing?

Are you striving to live as your beautifully created self, or are you hiding behind a mask?

What sins and failures are you still carrying around?

Can you bring them to the cross for forgiveness?

When will you meet with Me?

Are you willing to make our time a priority?

Can you be patient even if I don't give you all the answers you want right away?

Can you follow Me one step at a time?

f. Spend a few minutes in prayer—a real coaching session with the Holy Spirit. Think of all you learned in the past eight weeks. Look back at what you wrote on Week One, Day Four. What did you hope to gain through these forty days of spiritual renewal? How has your relationship with God grown over the past eight weeks? What do you want your spiritual life to look like going forward from here?

3. Lord, what truth do You want me to see today?

4. Write out this week's memory verse.

Day Three

REST

Let us therefore strive to enter that rest, so that no one may fall by the same sort of disobedience.
Hebrews 4:11

I am fascinated by the brain. This marvelous organ never ceases to amaze me. A few years ago, I attended a workshop where a professor from a major university told us of new findings in this area of study. Graduate students at his school were conducting research on the effect of sleep on the brain.

In the university studies, musicians were divided into two groups. Each group practiced a piano piece for a specified amount of time. After nine or ten hours, the musicians came back and played the piece they had previously worked on. Researchers observed mistakes and determined whether the performance was better, worse, or about the same as when they left the first practice session.

The one difference between the two groups was the time of day they performed the tests. One group first learned the piece in the morning and came back for evaluation in the evening. The other group first practiced in the evening, immediately went home and went to bed, and came back to perform the music in the morning.

Interestingly enough, the group that slept between their initial practice time and their performance consistently performed better than the other group. It turns out that while we are sleeping, our brains continue to learn. Although the fingers of the students were still, their brains were still practicing the piano piece. The university professor told us it is thought that sleep moves what we have learned during the day from short-term memory files to long-term memory banks.

Sleep is important to our brains.

I was thrilled to learn this. I love to snooze, but sometimes I feel guilty about needing rest. I could get so much more accomplished if my body didn't require eight hours of shut-eye. Now I have scientific proof that sleep is necessary.

God designed us with the need for rest. Our modern world tries to ignore this fact, as evidenced by Walmarts that never close and business executives who are expected to work eighty-hour weeks. In America, we try to deny the need for rest.

It may seem odd to talk about sleep and rest in a book about spiritual renewal. But think about it. When are you most likely to crack under pressure? When do you have a tendency to lose your temper? When do you forget to spend time with God? If you're like me, it's when you're tired and your energy reserves are pulled as tight as an overinflated birthday balloon. It only takes one pin prick of tension and everything explodes.

On the other hand, when are you more likely to be kind and patient? When are you able to respond with grace even in stressful situations? When do you hear God's comforting voice as you go through your day? Most likely these happen more consistently when you are rested. Rest for our bodies nurtures our souls.

Not only do our bodies need rest, but our minds need refreshing as well. Too often we rush from one appointment to the next, never giving our minds time to relax and recharge. Each day, do one thing that revives your energy for life: listen to music, read a book, or call a friend. Weave into your weeks and months activities that recharge you: window-shopping in an antiques store, attending a concert under the stars, taking a walk through the woods. These things may seem frivolous, but we need activities like these to keep our lives in balance.

Most important, our soul needs rest. Getting enough sleep and finding time for activities we love can help us to renew our souls. But rest is such an important requirement of the soul that God commands us to actively pursue it. Hebrews 4:11 says,

> Let us therefore strive to enter that rest, so that no one may fall
> by the same sort of disobedience.

It sounds like an oxymoron. How can we *strive* to enter rest? Wouldn't making every effort mean we aren't resting?

The only way it makes sense is if we know what kind of rest we are striving to enter. The author of Hebrews is talking about the rest that belongs to those who believe in the saving work of Jesus. The Greek word for "rest," *katapausis*, means "the heavenly blessedness in which God dwells," the place He promises to "persevering believers in Christ, partakers after the toils and trials of life on earth are ended."[45] Trusting in the cross of Christ means we don't need to *do* anything to enter heaven—a place of eternal rest from pain and hardship.

But Satan will continually try to get us to question this fact. It is his mission to cause us to doubt God's love for us. He subtly suggests that God couldn't possibly love us if we don't serve more people or make something of ourselves. He will continually prod us to do more to be "worthy."

So this is where the striving comes into play. We must make every effort to shut out Satan's lies and rest in the Savior's love. As baptized daughters of the Father, we have been washed clean in Jesus' blood. We don't need to work to obtain the rest of heaven, but it is a continual struggle to ignore Satan's ploys and enjoy the rest that is ours, even now, in Christ.

Jesus is saying, "Daughter, follow Me to a resting place. Shut out all those other voices that are telling you that you must perform a certain service or task to earn My love. Believe Me when I say there is nothing you can do to make Me love you more. Find time from the rush of the world to simply rest in My love. There is no other rest more necessary."

Slumber is necessary for our bodies. Sleep is necessary for optimum working of our brains. Rest is necessary for our souls.

Dearest Lord, thank You for Your saving work so that I can rest. Forgive me when I listen to Satan's lies and doubt Your love. Please help me to remember there is nothing I can do to make You love me more. Let me rest in Your peace. Amen.

Day Three

Soul Study

1. What is your reaction to the results of the study on the effects of sleep on piano performance?

2. Read Hebrews 4:1–13.
   a. How can we fall short of eternal rest (vv. 1–2)?

   b. How can you tell rest is important to God (vv. 3–4)?

   c. This passage talks about the failure of the Israelites to enter the rest of the Promised Land. Hebrews 3:18–19 tells more about their failure to enter God's rest. What prevented them from entering?

   d. Is there an area of unbelief that is holding you back from experiencing God's rest?

e. Hebrews 4:11 exhorts us to strive to enter that rest. Satan and the world are constantly trying to prevent us from entering God's rest. How will you strive to ignore their voices?

f. Verse 12 reminds us of a tool we can use to battle the forces keeping us from experiencing God's rest. What is that tool? How does it help us enter God's rest?

3. Lord, what truth do You want me to see today?

4. Write out this week's memory verse.

Day Four

SIMPLICITY

*You are anxious and troubled about
many things, but one thing is necessary.*
Luke 10:41—42

When my mother was growing up on a farm in Wisconsin, she had no need for a walk-in closet. She owned two dresses. Two. Life had a certain . . . simplicity.

I own more than two dresses. A lot more. In fact, I recently read the book *More or Less*[46] and took the author's challenge to take an inventory of my clothing. I began the exercise with a bit of trepidation because I do a lot of shopping at resale shops where I can spend twenty dollars and come home with a sack of twelve new-to-me items. My inventory revealed I owned six dresses (not bad). But my closet also held sixty-one T-shirts, twelve pairs of jeans, and seventy-eight sweaters! (I *counted* only twenty-four pairs of shoes because my husband has imposed a rule of no more than fifty shoes on my side of the closet.) This obvious excess motivated me to give away one-third of my clothes—but I can still hardly claim a simple lifestyle.

This complexity spills over into other areas of my life. In Week Five, I told you how I tend to agree to too many activities. My calendar becomes as jam-packed as my walk-in closet. My life is full—but not simple.

Why be concerned with simplicity anyway? What does limiting my possessions or my activities have to do with my spiritual life? Well, it's like this. Jesus told His friend Martha,

> You are anxious and troubled about many things, but one thing is necessary (Luke 10:41—42).

You can't make life more simple than that. One thing. Period.

Jesus is to be our one thing. Sitting in His presence should be our single-minded pursuit, as it was for Martha's sister Mary. That is true simplicity.

A calendar packed with activities and a house crammed full of stuff distracts us from our One thing. Every item we own requires time to wash it, file it, or polish it. Every activity we choose means time planning, driving, and participating. All of these things crowd out time to feed our souls through solitude, Bible study, and prayer. They all eat away at our time to sit at the feet of Jesus.

We are made to hunger for God, but the profusion of stuff can dull our appetite for His holy presence. Like junk food that can temporarily satisfy our rumbling stomachs without nourishing our bodies, our excessive belongings and time commitments can temporarily dull our soul cravings without giving our spirits what they need. As we wean ourselves from our dependence on possessions and relentless activity, we may feel an emptiness. But it is an emptiness God can fill.

Hanging onto a lot of stuff may mean our stuff has a hold on us. It's easy to get attached to our clothes, our homes, and our cool electronic toys. Like the man in Jesus' parable with a plentiful harvest, we build more and bigger barns to store our abundance. We build bigger garages, rent storage sheds, buy more shelving units and plastic bins. When I read the parable in Luke 12, I often wonder why the rich man didn't simply give the excess away. Then I realize—he's like me. He wants to keep it all for himself.

Clinging to our stuff can prevent us from sharing. Perhaps, the very reason I have an abundance is so I can provide for those who don't. A simple lifestyle encourages me to give away what I don't need. Keeping something because "I might need it someday" prevents me from sharing with someone who could use it now. Giving it away means trusting God will provide what I need when the time arises.

Obviously, I still have a long way to go in simplicity. Anyone who still owns fifty-four sweaters cannot claim to live a simple lifestyle. Maybe you can relate.

Jan Johnson writes in her *Spiritual Disciplines Companion*:

> As we practice simplicity, the Holy Spirit trains us to cut busyness and hurry out of our lives by remaining focused on God and God's kingdom. We refrain from participating in activities and owning possessions that are superfluous and do not further our union with God. The result is singleness of heart.[47]

This is not to say we cannot own fifty-four sweaters or two homes or three cars. Simplicity will look different for everyone. Living with a singleness of heart will mean asking ourselves questions like these:

☼ Do I need one more sweater, shirt, pair of shoes, book, activity, or appointment?

☼ Will adding this one more thing distract me from the One thing needed?

☼ Could someone else use something I have and don't currently need?

☼ Does purchasing this thing or adding this activity prevent me from giving to others as Christ is leading me to?

For most of us, simplicity will not mean going back to owning only two dresses. But it will mean evaluating what we have and what we purchase in terms of the effect it has on our relationship with the One who matters. Singleness of heart will mean frequent consultations with our Life Coach. He will let us know what activities to jettison from our lives to lighten our loads. He will show us what distractions we need to relinquish in order to have a truly abundant life.

Simplicity is the art of subtraction in order to add meaning to our lives.

Father in heaven, I confess my life is anything but simple. Too often, I am worried and upset about so many things that I ignore the One thing needed. Please show me what I need to give away, throw away, or stay away from in order to focus on You. In Jesus' name. Amen.

SOME SIMPLE WAYS TO PRACTICE SIMPLICITY

1. Reduce the number of clothes (or books or dishes or . . .) you own. Give them away to someone who can use them.

2. Post Jesus' words to Martha (Luke 10:41–42) in your closet or by your computer as a reminder to have a singleness of heart.

3. When you get one new sweater, pair of shoes, cooking utensil, and so on, get rid of an old one.

Soul Study

1. If you are brave enough, do an inventory of your own wardrobe.

CLOTHING ITEM	HOW MANY DO I OWN?
T-shirts	
Sweaters	
Jeans	
Pants	
Jackets	
Skirts	
Dresses	
Shoes	

2. Read the parable of the rich fool in Luke 12:13–21, understanding that Jesus calls us to depend on the riches of the Father's promises. Explore this passage with the SACRED reading process. After you have finished, write down anything you want to remember from this time.

    Silence your thoughts. (Allow your mind to quiet down.)

    Attend to the passage. (Read the passage out loud, pausing when the Spirit brings a part of it to your attention.)

    Contemplate the Word. (Meditate on the passage, asking, "How does this passage speak to my life?")

    Respond to the text. (Pray, pouring out your heart to God in response to what you have read.)

    Exhale and rest. (Read the text again and simply rest in the love of God.)

    Dwell in the Word. (Take a truth or promise with you into your day.)

3. Lord, what truth do You want me to see today?

4. Write out this week's memory verse.

Day Five

RULE OF LIFE

*Beloved, I pray that all may go well with you
and that you may be in good health, as it goes well
with your soul. 3 John 2*

Imagine Congress has passed a new law. Concerned with a population that is increasingly overweight and stressed, lawmakers came up with a plan to decrease health care costs. In order to reduce the incidence of heart disease, diabetes, and cancer, everyone in the country is required to spend one weekend a month at a health spa. Two days out of every month, citizens would eat healthy meals, practice new forms of exercise, and learn how to deal with stress. Hopefully, the effects of these twenty-four days would spill over into the other 341 days of the year.

Sounds good, right? (A rule that mandates that I don't have to cook twelve weekends of the year is one I could definitely support.) We know we should take care of our health, but we get so busy with work, school, and scrubbing floors that we often overlook the simple needs of our body—rest, nutritious food, and physical activity.

And if we tend to overlook the needs of our bodies, then we are even more likely to ignore the health of our souls. We careen through life, filling our hearts with spiritual junk food and our schedules with an overabundance of stress until our souls are so severely ill that they need to be put on life support.

During the past eight weeks, we have regularly visited the Soul Spa for God's healing touch. In the various rooms of the spa, we experienced soul renewal as we met with our Savior and allowed Him to refresh our hearts. My hope is that this time helped you reconnect with God in a way that has revitalized your spirit.

But we don't want to stop there. Just as one stay at a health spa probably won't change your eating habits for life, one visit to the Soul Spa will not automatically keep your soul from withering. Congress is unlikely to enact a law requiring a monthly stay at a spa and even more unlikely to require us to care for our spirits, but we can impose a rule on our own lives for soul upkeep. There is an ancient practice called Rule of Life that involves choosing spiritual habits to enhance your relationship with God.

At a health spa, you can take advantage of many different services and activities. During one visit, you might try a Pilates class to strengthen your core and a facial to deeply clean your skin. On the next stay, you might enjoy a massage and an appointment with a life coach to learn how to deal with stress.

During the past eight weeks, the Soul Spa has offered many "services" for your spirit. The Soul Spa menu included examen, solitude, Sabbath, and confession. You've explored hospitality, SACRED reading, fasting, and service. By now, you might even be feeling overwhelmed with the number of choices.

Just as you probably wouldn't engage in all that a spa has to offer in one visit, you probably won't practice all of these transformational exercises at the same time. The Rule of Life is a way of choosing what your soul needs *now*. You discern which habits will help you live closely with your Savior, which practices will help you become the person you are created to be.

As you fashion a Rule of Life for where you are at present, it is best to set aside a few hours to pray and listen to the Holy Spirit. One of my friends leaves work early one day a month to spend an afternoon at a coffee shop and establish her Rule of Life for the coming thirty days. Think of this time as a regular appointment with your spiritual Life Coach. As you read God's Word and pray, the Holy Spirit will lead you to the practices you most need right now. Some habits you will strive to practice daily, some monthly or yearly.

Create a balance in your Rule of Life. Choose practices that speak to deep desires in your soul. Perhaps you long to grow in prayer or to practice hospitality. But don't forget your soul's weaknesses or favorite sins—choose some habits that stretch you spiritually. You might recognize a need for simplicity or silence even though they aren't exactly what you want. Choose some solitary disciplines like meditation and some activities with the Body of Christ, such as fellowship.

When your Life Coach has directed you to the habits that breathe life into your soul, decide when and how you will practice them. Daily? Monthly? Yearly? Will you need someone else to practice them with? a mentor? a fellowship group? What will you need to practice them? A journal? Note cards?

As an example, I currently follow this Rule of Life: Every day, I engage in Bible study and prayer. Short-as-breath prayers help me center my thoughts on Christ throughout the day. I practice examen at night before I go to sleep, replaying the day in my mind, recalling God's presence with me. Where God shows me I have messed up in my words, in my thoughts, in my actions, I confess. I ask Him to forgive my known and unknown failures to obey His commandments.

Weekly, I worship with my congregation and participate in the Lord's Supper. I practice the Sabbath by resting and relaxing in the afternoon and avoiding technology.

Monthly, I want to practice the disciplines of solitude and mentoring. I plan on taking time to go to a park or sanctuary to spend extended time in God's Word. I also have a mentor who helps me develop professional goals and keeps me on track in my relationship with the Lord.

My prayer is that the Soul Spa experience has enriched your spiritual life. I hope the spa menu of practices we explored will help you care for your soul—the most important part of you. When your spirit is tired and worn, may this book become a resource for spiritual renewal.

Return to the Soul Spa again and again to meet with the God of restoration. Come when your soul is weary and your spirit aches for more. God invites you to bring your disappointments, your grief, and your brokenness. The Great Healer promises to miraculously transform your soul.

Holy and Everlasting God, I thank You that I can always come to You when my soul is shattered. You are the only One who can make the necessary repairs. Renew my spirit and restore my soul. Lead me to a deeper intimacy with You. In Jesus' name. Amen.

Day Five

Soul Study

1. How do you think a monthly trip to a spa would change your physical and mental health?

2. The apostle John wrote, "Beloved, I pray that all may go well with you and that you may be in good health, as it goes well with your soul" (3 John 2).
   a. How would you describe a healthy soul?

   b. How do you think God would describe a healthy soul? (Read Psalm 25:1–15, which describes the man whose "soul shall abide in well-being" [v. 13].)

3. Take some time to develop a Rule of Life for the coming month.
   a. Begin by asking the Holy Spirit to reveal the deepest needs of your soul. Do you most need a mentor to guide you? Do you long for solitude to listen to God? Do you sense a need for authenticity? Write the needs of your soul here.

b. Review the spiritual habits we have explored in the pages of Soul Spa. Choose one practice from each week that will help you meet the needs you wrote about above or a practice you simply want to explore further.

WEEK	SPIRITUAL DISCIPLINE I WANT TO EXPLORE	PRIORITY
ONE		
TWO		
THREE		
FOUR		
FIVE		
SIX		
SEVEN		
EIGHT		

c. Prioritize the above spiritual habits by numbering them 1–8, with 1 being the practice you feel most drawn to.

d. Establish a Rule of Life by filling out the plan below. Using the priorities above as a guide, choose one or two practices that you will do daily, one or two you will do weekly, and one or two that you will do monthly or yearly.

SPIRITUAL PRACTICE	HOW OFTEN I WILL DO IT	HOW AND WHEN I WILL DO IT
Example: A Soul Guide	Monthly	I will talk with my mentor once a month by telephone.

f. Write a prayer asking God to help you grow closer to Him as you practice these spiritual habits.

4. Lord, what truth do You want me to see today?

5. Write out this week's memory verse.

Group Activities

1. For your last Soul Spa meeting, once again create a spa atmosphere where you are meeting. Use some of the ideas on page 200 or incorporate some favorite spa activities: bring in a massage therapist with a massage chair, re-create the facial experience, or put out nail polish for manicures. You might set up different spa stations offering participants a variety of pampering choices.

2. An alternate idea for this last session would involve asking a Christian life coach to come and give a short talk on setting and achieving life goals.

3. Discuss the week's readings and Soul Studies. Allow each woman to choose one question that speaks to her heart. After she gives her answer, open up that question to the other members of the group. Ask some of the women to share their experience with the Spa Session activities from page 207.

4. Play some quiet worship music and ask each participant to design a Rule of Life for the coming month. Use the instructions on the previous page. If members of the group finished this exercise at home, ask them to use the time to pray about their plan and make any changes after further consultation with their Life Coach.

5. Give each person a note card and instruct participants to write down the obstacle they fear will keep them from following their plan. Divide into groups of two. Invite the partners to share their own Rule of Life and perceived hurdle. Partners will then exchange note cards and pray for each other. Encourage the women to connect with their partner in a week's time to see how they are progressing with their Rule of Life.

6. Close in a large group prayer.

7. Plan to meet in a month to see how you've grown through the Rule of Life you designed today.

PARTING THOUGHTS

God is a God of renovation. He longs to take our burdened, shattered, and sin-stained selves and make them new. The Father loves us so much He sent His Son that we might be restored. He has outlined a wonderful plan for us in His Word:

> "For all have sinned and fall short of the glory of God" (Romans 3:23).

No one is perfect. Everyone fails to meet God's standard of sinlessness. This sin prevents us from coming to Him and from entering heaven.

> "For God so loved the world, that He gave His only Son, that whoever believes in Him should not perish but have eternal life" (John 3:16).

God loved us so much that He sent His own Son to take the punishment we deserved for our sins and mistakes. Jesus' death enables us to live with God—forever.

> "For by grace you have been saved through faith. And this is not your own doing; it is the gift of God" (Ephesians 2:8).

God gives us faith to believe in Jesus. His grace and mercy save us from death.

> "But to all who did receive Him, who believed in His name, He gave the right to become children of God" (John 1:12).

By receiving Jesus in the waters of Baptism and the Holy Word of God, we become part of God's family.

I invite you to pray this prayer to the God who loves you and wants you to be part of His family:

Father in heaven, I realize that I am a sinner and fall short of what You want for my life. I know that I cannot save myself or earn eternal life. Thank You for sending Your Son, Jesus, to die for me. Through the power of His resurrection, You have made me alive eternally. Help me to turn from my sins and follow You. Thank You that although I may still fail, You will forgive me because Jesus paid the price for my sins. Thank You for Your gift of faith in Jesus, my Savior, and for the promise of eternal life with You. In Jesus' name I pray. Amen.

God speaks His words of love and grace to you. Through God's free gift of faith in Jesus, you now are part of God's family!

ANSWERS

Week One

DAY ONE: 1. Answers will vary. 2. Answers will vary. 3. Answers will vary. 4. a. We can exercise our powers of discernment by learning "to distinguish good from evil," helping us to become mature Christians. b. Punishment and instruction can train us. This training may not be pleasant but will result in peace and righteousness. c. Because our hearts can be trained by greed and other evil influences, we must guard our hearts. d. Answers will vary. One possible answer: Exercise your heart by learning to distinguish good from evil and regarding hard times as heart training. Be careful not to exercise in evil. 5. Memory verse. DAY TWO: 1. Answers will vary, but might include a long-term physical training program increases strength and endurance, improving overall health. 2. Answers will vary. 3. a. Examples: Take my body to worship service. Use my gifts to serve others. Kneel in worship. Sing. Sexual purity. b. Answers will vary. c. Answers will vary, but might include advertising, media attention given to the rich and famous, Facebook, busyness. d. Answers will vary. 4. Memory verse. DAY THREE: 1. Answers will vary. 2. Answers will vary. 3. a. Answers will vary. b. Answers will vary. c. Answers will vary. d. Deuteronomy 31:6—God will never leave us; He always goes with us. Psalm 136:1—God is good. His love endures forever. Psalm 23:1—God cares for me like a shepherd. He knows my needs. 4. Memory verse. DAY FOUR: 1. Answers will vary. 2. a. His soul faints for the Lord. His heart cries out for God. b. Word pictures include fainting and birds building a nest near God's altar. c. Those who dwell in God's house and those whose hearts are highways to Zion are blessed. d. Answers will vary. e. Answers will vary, but might include the realization that one day spent praising God and soaking up His presence is better than a thousand anywhere else. 3. Memory verse. DAY FIVE: 1. Answers will vary. 2. a. He revives our souls. b. He guards our souls. c. He cheers our souls. d. He satisfies souls. e. He gives our souls rest. 3. Answers will vary. 4. Memory verse.

Week Two

DAY ONE: 1. Answers will vary. 2. Answers will vary. 3. Answers will vary. 4. a. Answers will vary. b. Answers will vary. c. Answers will vary. d. Answers will vary. 5. Memory verse. DAY TWO: 1. Answers will vary. 2. Answers will vary. 3. a. Answers will vary, but might include walking closely with Jesus means walking in meekness, mercy, and purity. b. Answers will vary, but might include walking with Jesus means living a life very different from the rest of the world. c. Answers will vary. d. Answers will vary. 4. Answers will vary. 5. Memory verse. DAY THREE: 1. Answers will vary. 2. Answers will vary. 3. Answers will vary. 4. Answers will vary. 5. Memory verse. DAY FOUR: 1. Answers will vary. 2. Answers will vary. 3. a. God's Word in our hearts helps us not to slip and fall. b. God's Word in our hearts helps us to delight in God's will. c. Memorizing God's Word helps us obey God and avoid sin. d. God's Word in our hearts helps us not to fear men. 4. Answers will vary. 5. Memory verse. DAY FIVE: 1. Answers will vary. 2. Answers will vary. 3. Answers will vary. 4. Memory verse.

Week Three

DAY ONE: 1. Answers will vary. 2. Answers will vary. 3. a. Events of Jesus' Hectic Day: teaching in the synagogue, healing a man with an unclean spirit, healing Simon's mother-in-law, going out to the townspeople—healing them and casting out demons. b. Answers will vary. c. Answers will vary. d. Jesus got up very early in the morning and went to "a desolate place" to pray. e. Time alone with His Father seemed to give Jesus new energy and a refocused purpose. f. Answers will vary. 4. Answers will vary. 5. Memory verse.

DAY TWO: 1. Answers will vary. 2. a. Mount Horeb is called Mount of God and is another name for Mount Sinai where Moses met God. Perhaps Elijah thought going there would bring him closer to God. b. Answers will vary. c. Answers will vary. d. Answers will vary, but might include God gave Elijah what he needed in the form of practical advice. God told him that at least seven thousand people got his message. He was not as alone as he thought. This helps me realize that God is not angry when I express my feelings and will give me what I need. 3. Answers will vary. 4. Memory verse. DAY THREE: 1. Answers will vary. 2. Answers will vary. 3. Answers will vary. 4. Answers will vary. 5. Memory verse. DAY FOUR: 1. Answers will vary. 2. a. Moses asked God to show His ways, that God would go with them, and that God would show His glory. b. Answers will vary. c. God's promise is "My presence will go with you, and I will give you rest." d. God's presence comforts us and protects us. When we are aware of His presence and love, we realize that we don't have to work to earn His approval and the need for the approval of other people loosens its grip on us. e. Moses saw God's goodness. He did not see God's face. f. Answers will vary. 3. Answers will vary. 4. Answers will vary. 5. Memory verse. DAY FIVE: 1. Answers will vary. 2. Answers will vary. 3. a. Some phrases of despair: "My tears have been my food" (v. 3); "My soul is cast down within me" (v. 5); "I say to God, my rock: 'Why have You forgotten me?'" (v. 9); and "a deadly wound in my bones" (v. 10). Some phrases of hope: "I remember . . . how I would go with the throng . . . to the house of God" (v. 4); "glad shouts and songs of praise" (v. 4); "Hope in God; for I shall again praise Him" (v. 5); and "By day the LORD commands His steadfast love" (v. 8). b. Answers may vary, but might include it helps us see that we don't have to "pretty things up" for God. We can be totally honest with Him. c. Answers will vary. 4. Answers will vary. 5. Memory verse.

Week Four

DAY ONE: 1. Answers will vary. 2. Answers will vary. 3. Answers will vary. 4. Memory verse. DAY TWO: 1. Answers will vary. 2. a. The issue was where to worship. The Samaritans worshiped on the mountain; the Jews worshiped in Jerusalem. b. Jesus told her that there would be a time when people would not worship in either place. c. The most important element is to worship in spirit and truth. d. Answers will vary, but might include types of music, liturgy or no liturgy, or style of sanctuary. e. The outward form of worship is not that important. What God wants is true worship, allowing the Holy Spirit to draw us to God. f. Answers will vary. 3. Answers will vary. 4. Memory verse. DAY THREE: 1. Answers will vary. 2. a. Answers will vary. b. Answers will vary, but might include it was the last night that He could institute the Lord's Supper before He literally gave up His body and blood. He gave the disciples a tangible way to remember that sacrifice. He is the Paschal Lamb, sacrificed for us; He reinforced this truth at Passover, when a lamb was sacrificed. c. Answers will vary, but might include read the Gospel accounts of the Last Supper, mindfully participate in the confession of sins and absolution, or engage your senses when you partake of the bread and wine. 3. Answers will vary. 4. Memory verse. DAY FOUR: 1. Answers will vary. 2. Answers will vary. 3. a. God rested on the Sabbath day. He made it holy. b. God thinks Sabbath is important enough to make it one of the Ten Commandments. The Israelites were not to work on that day, but rest. As New Testament Christians, we keep this command because God knows we need rest and time in His Word. c. God blesses all who keep the Sabbath. He promises, "I will . . . make them joyful in My house of prayer" (v. 7). d. God created the Sabbath for man. He knows we need rest and renewal. 4. Answers will vary. 5. Memory verse. DAY FIVE: 1. Answers will vary. 2. Answers will vary. 3. a. The father thought his son was dead but found out he was alive. b. The celebration included party clothes (the best robes, ring, and shoes), lots of food (fattened calf), and revelry (music and dancing). c. Over the top. Going all out. A good time was had by (almost) all. d. Our Father is a generous God who loves to celebrate and lavish us with His love. e. Answers will vary. f. Answers will vary. 4. Answers will vary. 5. Answers will vary. 6. Memory verse.

Week Five

DAY ONE: 1. Answers will vary. 2. Answers will vary. 3. a. From His model of humility, the disciples instinctively knew that He wouldn't approve of trying to be the greatest. b. It can help us because He already knows and loves our real self. He knows our anxious, rebellious, and prideful thoughts, but is always ready to forgive. When we try to hide something, it rarely gets better. When we admit our faults, which Jesus already knows, He can forgive them. The Spirit can restore us. c. Answers will vary, but many will find it difficult to "turn and become like children" because it involves humility and dependence on others. d. childlike: definition—resembling a child, trusting and candid; characteristic or behavior—trusting those who care for him, speaking honestly and openly; how this affects my relationship with God—if we have childlike trust, we are less likely to doubt God's goodness; childlike honesty may enable us to be open with God about our failures and fears. childish: definition—immature; characteristic or behavior—stubbornness, impatience, temper tantrums; how this affects my relationship with God—when we stubbornly want our own way, we block our relationship with God and the peace He offers. 4. Answers will vary. 5. Memory verse. DAY TWO: 1. Answers will vary. 2. Answers will vary. 3. a. Answers will vary. b. Answers will vary. c. Answers will vary. 4. Answers will vary. 5. Memory verse. DAY THREE: 1. Answers will vary. 2. Answers will vary. 3. a. Answers will vary. b. Answers will vary, but because of Christ's atoning work on the cross, He sees us as loved daughters, forgiven, righteous, and pure. c. Answers will vary. d. Answers will vary. e. Answers will vary. 4. Answers will vary. 5. Memory verse. DAY FOUR: 1. Answers will vary. 2. Answers will vary. 3. Answers will vary. 4. Answers will vary. 5. Answers will vary. 6. Memory verse. DAY FIVE: 1. Answers will vary. 2. Answers will vary. 3. a. Jesus instructs us to do three things in secret: give to the needy, pray, and fast. b. Although giving, praying, and fasting can be done for God alone, we can be tempted to give more or pray longer prayers or talk about our fasting practices simply for attention from people. "Your Father who sees in secret will reward you" (v. 4). c. Answers will vary. d. Doing them secretly helps us do them for the Lord and not for the approval of people. This same attitude of humility can carry over when we give, pray, or fast publicly. 4. Answers will vary. 5. Memory verse.

Week Six

DAY ONE: 1. Answers will vary. 2. Answers will vary. 3. a. Answers will vary. b. Answers will vary. c. Answers will vary. d. Answers will vary. 4. Answers will vary. 5. Memory verse. DAY TWO: 1. Answers will vary. 2. a. Answers will vary. b. Answers will vary. c. In serving, we think of others' needs as more important than our own. We learn to put ourselves in a lower position. Being served may also teach humility; if we are not accustomed to needing help, it can be hard to accept it. 3. Answers will vary. 4. Memory verse. DAY THREE: 1. Answers will vary. 2. Answers will vary. 3. a. Some phrases include "let love be genuine" (v. 9)"; "love one another with brotherly affection" (v. 10); "outdo one another in showing honor" (v. 10); "serve the Lord" (v. 11); "contribute to the needs of the saints" (v. 13); "seek to show hospitality" (v. 13); and "live in harmony with one another" (v. 16). b. Answers will vary. c. Hospitality that shows sincere love pays more attention to the people than the food or fancy presentation. Sincere love welcomes people with open arms. Insincere hospitality has fancy dishes and gourmet food—but is clearly done to impress. Insincere love is so busy with preparations it has no time for the guests. d. Some ways you can show love to strangers without inviting them to your home include give to organizations that help the homeless, volunteer at a homeless shelter, teach GED or ESL classes, and give to relief organizations. 4. Answers will vary. 5. Memory verse. DAY FOUR: 1. Answers will vary. 2. Answers will vary, but may include personality differences, fear of opening up, differing opinions in worship practice, pride, or not listening well. 3. Answers will vary. 4. Answers will vary. 5. Memory verse. DAY FIVE: 1. Answers will vary. 2. Answers will vary. 3. a. Answers will vary. b. Answers will vary. c. Elizabeth's baby leaped in her womb and she was filled with the Holy Spirit. God told her the good news! d. Answers will vary, but might include it was probably comforting to receive confirmation of Gabriel's message from someone else. It might have been a relief to not need to find words to tell Elizabeth of her unbelievable news. e. Answers will vary. 4. Answers will vary. 5. Memory verse.

Week Seven

DAY ONE: 1. Answers will vary. 2. a. Answers will vary. b. Answers will vary. c. Answers will vary. d. Watching is being alert to Satan's subtle attacks. Watching helps us avoid temptation like watching for holes in the path we are walking on—helps us avoid falling. Praying calls on the power of God. Alone it is difficult, even impossible to avoid temptation, but God is much more powerful than Satan. e. Answers will vary. 3. Answers will vary. 4. Memory verse. DAY TWO: 1. The harder our bodies work, the more air they need. We often sense a greater need for prayer when life is hard. 2. Answers will vary. 3. Answers will vary, but may include: Jesus taught us to "always pray and not lose heart" (v.1). He wants us to be persistent in prayer. But we know that God does not listen to our prayers because of our persistence; He hears us because of His love for us in Christ Jesus. 4. Answers will vary. 5. Memory verse. DAY THREE: 1. Answers will vary. 2. a. Joel encouraged the people to fast and pray that God would spare His people. b. Fasting would be a visible sign of repentance, that God's people were returning to Him. c. As we experience hunger, we are reminded of our human weakness and dependence on God. It is in that state of vulnerability and humility that we are more open to the Holy Spirit's tender work in our hearts. d. Characteristics of God: gracious, compassionate, slow to anger, abounding in love, relenting from sending calamity. e. We remember that God is not manipulated by a fast—He is already compassionate and loving. God's grace enables us to fast from earthly things. f. Answers will vary. 3. Answers will vary. 4. Memory verse. DAY FOUR: 1. Answers will vary. 2. Answers will vary. 3. a. Answers will vary. b. Answers will vary. c. i. That God would strengthen them with power (v. 16). ii. That Christ would dwell in their hearts through faith (v. 17). iii. That they would have the power to grasp the extent of God's love (v. 18). iv. That they would experience the love that surpasses knowledge (v. 19). v. That they would be filled with the fullness of God (v. 19). vi. That God would be glorified through what He does in their lives (v. 21). d. Answers will vary. 4. Answers will vary. 5. Memory verse. DAY FIVE: 1. Answers will vary. 2. a. Perhaps, they saw an openness or a fervency or an intimacy that was lacking in their prayer life. b. The first story encourages us to ask boldly because God will give us whatever we need. The second story lets us know we have a Father in heaven who loves to give good gifts. c. Answers will vary. 3. Answers will vary. 4. Memory verse.

Week Eight

DAY ONE: 1. Answers will vary, but may include he realized there was more to this life than fishing and making a living. 2. a. Answers will vary. b. Answers will vary. c. Peter obeyed because it was Jesus' word. He did it because Jesus asked him to. d. Answers will vary. e. Answers will vary. f. Answers will vary. 3. Answers will vary. 4. Memory verse. DAY TWO: 1. Answers will vary. 2. In the ESV, Jesus calls the Holy Spirit "Helper." b. Answers will vary. c. Jesus said the Holy Spirit will convict the world "concerning sin, because they do not believe in [Him]." d. Answers will vary. e. Answers will vary. f. Answers will vary. 3. Answers will vary. 4. Memory verse. DAY THREE: 1. Answers will vary. 2. a. We fall short of eternal rest if we don't receive God's good news of grace in faith. b. God rested on the seventh day because His work of creation was finished. His people are also free to enter His rest and peace. c. The Israelites were unable to enter the Promised Land because of disobedience and unbelief. d. Answers will vary. e. Answers will vary. f. The Word of God is the tool we can use. It shows the thoughts and attitudes that are preventing us from entering God's rest. It continually reassures us of God's grace. 3. Answers will vary. 4. Memory verse. DAY FOUR: 1. Answers will vary. 2. Answers will vary. 3. Answers will vary. 4. Memory verse. DAY FIVE: 1. Answers will vary. 2. a. Answers will vary. b. A healthy soul trusts in the Lord, waits for God, and seeks Him for guidance. A healthy soul clings to the steadfast love and faithfulness of the Lord. A healthy soul fears the Lord and comes to God for forgiveness. The healthy soul enjoys friendship with the Lord. 3. Answers will vary. 4. Answers will vary. 5. Memory verse.

END NOTES

1. blueletterbible.org/lang/lexicon/lexicon.cfm?Strongs=G1128&t=KJV, August 16, 2014.

2. Rick Renner, *Sparkling Gems from the Greek* (Tulsa, OK: Teach All Nations, 21st printing, 2003), 874.

3. Spiros Zodhiates Th.D., *The Complete Word Study Dictionary: New Testament* (Chattanooga, TN: AMG Publishers, 1992), 683.

4. John W. Kleinig, *Grace Upon Grace: Spirituality for Today* (St. Louis, MO Concordia Publishing House, 2008), 10.

5. blueletterbible.org/lang/lexicon/lexicon.cfm?Strongs=G1679&t=KJV, August 21, 2014.

6. Kleinig, 11.

7. Adele Ahlberg Calhoun, *Spiritual Disciplines Handbook* (Downers Grove, IL: InterVarsity Press, 2005), Kindle Edition, Introduction, 179-188 of 3484.

8. Calhoun, Introduction, 198 of 3484.

9. Martin Luther, *A Simple Way to Pray* (St. Louis, MO: Concordia Publishing House, 2012).

10. Kleinig, 14–15.

11. blueletterbible.org/lang/lexicon/lexicon.cfm?Strongs=G5590&t=KJV, August 28, 2014.

12. johnortberg.com/book_type/books, August 28, 2014.

13. Jeanne Guyon, *Experiencing the Depths of Jesus Christ* (Beaumont, TX: SeedSowers, 1973), 11, quoted by Jan Johnson in *Spiritual Disciplines Companion* (Downers Grove, IL: InterVarsity Press, 2009), 133.

14. Kleinig, 96.

15. Kleinig, 102.

16. twopaths.com/faq_WordCount, June 23, 2014.

17. Kleinig, 19.

18. heartlandspa.com/recipes. June 23, 2014.

19. John Baillie, *A Diary of Private Prayer* (New York: Charles Scribner's Sons, 1949), 57. books.google.com/books?id=FFRClmctEC8C&pg=PA57&lpg=PA57&dq=When+thou+dost+knock+at+my+heart%27s+door&source=bl&ots=L5TKY-nzH0&sig=uRgdS3t-Y0ObfZqlLuUttUld9Tg&hl=en&sa=X&ei=hNFsVJOUA8ayyASe9IGYBA&ved=0CCAQ6AEwAA#v=onepage&q=When%20thou%20dost%20knock%20at%20my%20heart%27s%20door&f=false, November 19, 2014.

20. articles.latimes.com/2013/jul/13/health/la-he-spa-spirit-20130713, August 2, 2014.

21. cyberhymnal.org/htm/r/e/rejtlord, August 2, 2014.

22. blueletterbible.org/lang/lexicon/lexicon.cfm?Strongs=G1392&t=KJV, July 8, 2014.

23. blueletterbible.org/lang/lexicon/lexicon.cfm?Strongs=G4151&t=KJV, July 9, 2014.

24. blueletterbible.org/lang/lexicon/lexicon.cfm?Strongs=G225&t=KJV, July 9, 2014.

25. hebrew4christians.com/Holidays/Spring_Holidays/Unleavened_Bread/Anavah/anavah, July 24, 2014.

26. hebrew4christians.com/Holidays/Spring_Holidays/Pesach/Seder/Kadesh/kadesh, July 23, 2014.

27. Note: In the ESV, the verse reads, "you shall celebrate the feast of the LORD seven days. On the first day shall be a solemn rest, and on the eighth day shall be a solemn rest." The Hebrew for solemn here is *shabbathown*, which means "Sabbath."

28. blueletterbible.org/lang/lexicon/lexicon.cfm?Strongs=H2287&t=KJV, August 1, 2014.

29. Donna Pyle, *Quenched: Christ's Living Water for a Thirsty Soul* (St. Louis, MO: Concordia Publishing House, 2014), Kindle Edition 2575 of 3221.

30. Quoted in David G. Benner, *The Gift of Being Yourself: The Sacred Call to Self-Discovery* (Downers Grove, IL: InterVarsity Press, 2004), 20.

31. brainyquote.com/quotes/quotes/e/eecummin161592, October 7, 2014.

32. *Concordia: The Lutheran Confessions*, second edition (St. Louis: Concordia Publishing House, 2006), LC III 30.

33. blueletterbible.org/lang/lexicon/lexicon.cfm?Strongs=H5564&t=KJV, January 22, 2015.

34. Dallas Willard, *The Spirit of the Disciplines: Understanding How God Changes Lives* (San Francisco: HarperSanFrancisco, 1988), 173.

35. Robert Mulholland, *Invitation to a Journey* (Downers Grove, IL: InterVarsity Press, 1993), 154, quoted in *Spiritual Disciplines Companion* by Jan Johnson (Downers Grove, IL: IVP Books, 2009), 155.

36. Kelli B. Trujillo, *The Busy Mom's Guide to Spiritual Survival* (Indianapolis, Indiana: Wesleyan Publishing House, 2007), Kindle edition, Chapter 10, 1324 of 1739.

37. brainyquote.com/quotes/quotes/m/martinluth385793, October 21, 2014.

38. *Concordia*, LC III 30.

39. stress.org/take-a-deep-breath, October 16, 2014

40. brainyquote.com/quotes/quotes/m/martinluth385793, October 21, 2014.

41. dictionary.reference.com/browse/intercession?s=t, October 20, 2014.

42. *Concordia*, LC III 22.

43. Dietrich Bonhoeffer, quoted in *Word: God Speaks to Us*, by John T. Pless (St. Louis: Concordia Publishing House, 2006), 28.

44. Kleinig, 108.

45. blueletterbible.org/lang/lexicon/lexicon.cfm?Strongs=G2663&t=KJV, November 4, 2014.

46. Jeff Shinabarger, *More or Less: Choosing a Lifestyle of Excessive Generosity* (Colorado Springs: David C. Cook, 2013).

47. Jan Johnson, *Spiritual Disciplines Companion* (Downers Grove, IL: InterVarsity Press, 2009), 227.

ACKNOWLEDGMENTS

Thank you

to John, who is the most wonderful life-partner, hand-holder, tension-lifter, humor-provider, and computer-fixer a writer could have;

to Anna and Nate, Nathaniel and Mary, who bring so much joy to our family;

to Aaron, Andrew, and Alexander, who provide just the right mix of delight and mischief in our lives;

to all the people at Concordia Publishing House who have given me the opportunity to serve women with my words;

to Peggy Kuethe, my amazing editor and cherished friend;

to Jan, Lara, and Suzanne, who read (and improved!) many pages of this book in its early stages;

to Rhonda, Sue, and Pam, who journeyed to the Soul Spa with me every Wednesday night for months;

to the people of Hope who have faithfully walked through a deep valley with us this year;

to my mother, who inspired my love of God's Word by giving me a Living Bible and who continues to be the best PR agent a girl could have;

and most of all, to Jesus, who holds me together every single day.